Crazy,

So nice to meet you, thanks for all the support.

Take care my friend!

al
Dy

THE LIFE OF A HOTELIER

(THE GM YEARS)

THE LIFE OF A HOTELIER

(THE GM YEARS)

AL DEBERRY

Clovercroft/Publishing

The Life of a Hotelier

©2020 by Al DeBerry

Published by Clovercroft Publishing, Franklin, Tennessee

Edited by David Brown

Cover Design by Marco Mauro

Interior Design by Suzanne Lawing

Printed in the United States of America

ISBN 978-1-950892-59-4

AL DEBERRY

Al is a seasoned hotelier with more than thirty years' experience in the hotel industry. He started in the business while attending the University of North Texas before advancing to assistant general manager. He quickly then became a general manager of his first hotel soon after his twenty-first birthday. He served as GM for the next eight years at two different hotels in Texas. Following his career as a GM, Al went on to have a fifteen-year career as an area director, overseeing a total of thirty-eight hotels in multiple cities throughout Texas and Colorado.

Upon leaving his role as area director, he invested in a partnership to buy a hotel in Wisconsin, and as Al says, "I was blessed to be able to buy a hotel, which is the dream of many people in the hotel business. So I checked that one off of my bucket list, and I could not have enjoyed the experience of hotel ownership any more than I did."

After a few years, Al sold his part of the hotel back to his partners. He ultimately created and developed The Hotel Association, a locally based hotel organization for the hotel community in the Dallas/Fort Worth metroplex (DFW metroplex). He had discovered his real passion for the business by giving back to the industry that had been so good to him.

Al was involved with different hospitality related associations, including the Texas Hotel and Lodging Association (TH&LA) where he served on the board of directors from 1997–2014 and was chairman of the board for TH&LA in 2009. He was involved with the

Hotel Association of Tarrant County (HATC) serving on the board of directors from 2004–2014 and as president of HATC in 2010 and 2011. Later, while overseeing The Hotel Association he had founded, he served on the board of directors for the Texas Travel Industry Association (TTIA) starting in 2016, moving up to the executive committee of TTIA within two years. Al was named as the 2010 State of Texas Leadership Award winner by the American Hotel & Lodging Association. He was appointed to the hospitality committee of the Super Bowl XLV Host Committee in the DFW metroplex from early 2009 until the Super Bowl in Arlington, Texas, on February 6, 2011.

This book, *The Life of a Hotelier, the GM Years* was written by Al DeBerry after having experienced many years in the hotel industry. He has seen it from all sides and angles. This book gives you a behind-the-scenes look at what Al saw as he literally grew up in the hotel business over the course of his first few years in the business. Many hoteliers encounter similar situations every day, but most guests never see or hear about these stories to know what amazing professionals the people in the hotel industry are.

The hotel business is a fast-paced life where days run into weeks, weeks into months, and months into years. The doors never close, and the guests keep coming. Addresses of the players in the game may change and the employees may change, but people in the hotel industry would not think of having a career in any other profession. They love the business that much, and certainly Al does as well.

Enjoy the book. Hopefully it resonates at some level for you regardless of what industry you are in!

To my beloved mother, Elizabeth DeBerry, who inspired me,
motivated me, and kept my life balanced.

CONTENTS

1

1985 – TURNING INTO A NIGHT OWL.

I knew I was going to run out of money soon. My savings were vanishing quickly and school was on the horizon as I was set to continue my college career that upcoming fall. I had quit my job working at a movie theater at the beginning of summer in 1985 after finishing my freshman year of college at the University of North Texas (then known as North Texas State University) in Denton, Texas.

As a nineteen-year-old young college student, I needed a job and needed it quickly in August before school started back again in September. This was in those days before any type of the online job searches or the websites we have now. You had to look through the newspaper for any employment in the help wanted ads. As a kid growing up in Denton (located about thirty miles north of Dallas with a population then of about fifty thousand people), there were basically three newspapers that I knew of to look for a job: the hometown *Denton Record Chronicle, The Dallas Morning News*, and *The Dallas Time Herald.*

Growing up, I had always been a night owl. My morning classes had started at 8:00 a.m. the previous semester, so I knew I wanted none of that this time around. My first "real" job in high school had been at the local movie theater in Denton, which was usually evenings and late nights. For this new job opportunity, I did not want to work evenings or weekends if at all possible.

As I continued to search the newspapers for a job, a help wanted ad stood out to me, and it read, "Overnight front desk position at hotel from 11:00 p.m.–7:00 a.m. Looking for independent, self-driven person with basic math aptitude and outgoing personality. The position is for a full-time night auditor, Sunday through Thursday." I thought, well that sounds pretty good. Even though I believed I did have an outgoing personality, I thought how many people would I actually see from 11:00 p.m.–7:00 a.m.? There certainly would not be much interaction with other people, would there? Well, as people in the hotel business can understand, the night shift position is where the fun begins because the people you interact with during those eight crazy hours makes it the most interesting shift of the day.

I decided I would take a shot at this opportunity and go to the hotel, fill out the application, and see if I could learn more about what this "full-time night auditor" position actually meant. Again, in those days, you went to the place where the job was located, you filled out a real application on paper, and you met with someone in person. There were no online databases or websites to create personal profiles like everyone goes through in today's world to get a job. I thought maybe I would go to the hotel around 10:00 a.m. because the manager of the hotel should be in by then (again, my perception at the time), so I could meet with the manager and hopefully get the job. I was correct about the manager coming in around 10:00 a.m. (more on that later) but as I walk in the door, I am greeted by the young lady at the front desk of the hotel who just happens to be one of my really good friends from school who I have known since seventh grade.

Getting the opportunity rolling is reasonably correct because my friend Lisa was truly excited to catch up, as we had not seen each other since our class graduated Denton High School in 1984. It seemed like she had plenty of time to talk. She came out to the lobby right away. There appeared to be no manager at the hotel, plus the phone never seemed to ring the entire time I was there for maybe forty-five minutes to an hour. She said the manager was not in at the time and he would not be back until the afternoon. He had just gone home and was sleeping because he was filling in for the "night auditor" position that I was now applying for. My thought was, okay, the guy is probably desperate. He is stuck working this awful overnight position, and I actually would very much like the job.

After completing the job application, I went to lunch with another high school buddy of mine, and told him about the job. He said he thought I could do it from what I was telling him, but was worried about me going to college at the same time as holding a full-time job, especially an overnight shift with those hours. I told him it would work out because I am always awake late in the evening, plus I might be able to do my college homework while I was working. Again who is going to be at the hotel from 11:00 p.m.–7:00 a.m.? The guests should all be asleep, and apparently, I just have to do some paperwork for this job during my shift, which should not be a problem.

The following day, after I had filled out my application, sure enough Lisa called me from the hotel. I was not home at the time, but she left a message on the answering machine. We had the reel-to-reel type of answering machine, and luckily, this day it was working (sometimes it would stop working completely). Lisa left a message for me to call her right away. I returned the call, and the manager wanted me to come in for an interview the following day. The next day was Friday, and he wanted me to come in early because he would be working the night audit shift on that Thursday night. So I needed to get there to meet him before he went home to get some rest. So, I was all set for my big interview on that Friday morning at 7:30 a.m.

My mother was completely against the idea and thought I was wasting my time even going for the interview. She felt I needed to focus on college and not fool around with a full-time job where I would be alone all night by myself with no one there to work with. I told her it may not even work out, but I needed to go and hear what the manager had to say. It was a full-time job that paid $5.00 an hour, and in my mind, that is $200.00 a week, $800.00 a month, more than enough for a college kid with no "real" bills living at home and going to college. My mom was not convinced, but she finally agreed that I should go take a look to find out more about the job, but I was NOT to take the job on this day even if he offered it to me on the spot. Sorry, Mom, that was not going to happen, as my money was draining and I needed some cash in my pocket right away.

I arrived for the interview. The manager looked tired and completely out of sorts as you can imagine with him running the hotel while also working this crazy 11:00 p.m.–7:00 a.m. shift five days a week. That would give me forty hours full-time, but I would essentially have a three-day weekend to do whatever I wanted with my buddies.

My previous job at the movie theater had always included Friday and Saturday nights. So having the weekends to do as I pleased was definitely something that interested me. At the movie theater, I had made minimum wage ($3.35 per hour). I never received a raise during the two and a half years I had worked there through high school. Getting paid $5.00 an hour was really appealing. In 1985, the United States' economy was somewhat sluggish with the savings and loan crisis on the horizon. This would play a part in my future understanding of the economy, but at the time, I just knew jobs were hard to come by and a good one making $5.00 an hour, plus being full-time, was something I needed and certainly wanted.

I met with the manager of the hotel for the job. He had some basic interview questions. He asked about my job at the movie theater and my relationship with Lisa at the front desk. He also inquired about my connection to Denton, how long I had lived there, and what were my plans for college and beyond. It was a good start to the interview. Then he said Lisa had told him I was really good at math (whether I was or not was up for interpretation at that point in my life). Apparently the night auditor position had a lot to do with math, so Lisa knew if she said that, it could give me a real chance to get hired.

The interview went for about an hour or so, and I could tell he was starting to get tired. Remember, he had been up maybe since 9 p.m. the night before and we were now closing in on 9 a.m. that morning. He then said, okay, based on Lisa's recommendation and that he was tired of doing the job, if I wanted the job, it was mine, and could I start that Sunday at 11:00 p.m.? I said, "Of course, I'm in" (totally against my mother's wishes). I was going to start that new endeavor on Sunday night, August 11, 1985. Even though I of course did not know it at that moment, my life would never be the same. As you can imagine, my mom was not too happy when I went to see her at work that day to say I had taken the job. I was really excited about what was about to happen because I felt at the time a job paying $5.00 an hour was A LOT of money for a college kid to have. So let's get started. It is going to be great!

Oh, as a sidenote, I was told many years later that my mother had told her co-workers and her friends when I took the job that she thought it was the dumbest thing I could have done. Working those hours, 11:00 p.m.–7:00 a.m., would wear me down and I would not last more than a week. Now, these many years later, even after her passing away in 2015, I still get a sense of pride knowing how much she wanted to protect me, but how wrong she was at the time. It all came together with Lisa's help and the manager being exhausted on that particular day, allowing me to get into this crazy hotel business. Thus I was starting the life of a hotelier.

I was so excited about starting the first night, I had taken a quick nap that Sunday afternoon, but got up around 6:00 p.m., had dinner with my mom, and then got ready for my first official night in the hotel business. It was supposed to be a normal night, nothing special about the day or the weather. I drove up to the hotel around 10:45 p.m., as I wanted to make sure no matter what I was on time. I also wanted to meet anyone who was working. Turns out it was just the 3:00 p.m.–11:00 p.m. clerk on duty. She was very nice when I met her. She was expecting me, so she showed me where to clock in. The part-time weekend night auditor was coming in to train me. He showed up right at 11:00 p.m., and I was ready to learn the new job.

But, as it happens, these things can come with some twists and turns. The first twist took about an hour to happen that first night. I was standing at the front desk learning how to do check-ins. A lady comes in and asks me if I can help her husband, as he had an oxygen tank in their car that was too heavy to carry in alone. Not sure why they were traveling with such a large oxygen tank on the road, but, again, in 1985 things were different. I was not judging, just happy to help out, so I ask the guy I was training with if I can go to their car. He says yes, and I head out to the car with this nice lady to help with her husband's oxygen tank. Well, the thing looks like a small nuclear bomb. It is somehow propped up in the back seat, and saying it was heavy was definitely an understatement. Heck, I didn't really know what workers' comp was at the time, but if I had known, it may have been in the back of my mind, as I was about to start with the under-taking of carrying this dreaded oxygen tank.

Remember, I got the job because of Lisa's help and my "math skills." No one said anything about carrying someone's one hundred pound oxygen tank from their car to their hotel room, alone, around midnight. There was no luggage cart and there was no maintenance cart. This was me vs. the oxygen tank, and it was not going to get the best of me. The fight was on! I managed to get the tank out of the car, lug it around like I was a deep sea diver from *National Geographic*, and thankfully, the guy training me on the front desk had put the couple in a room on the first floor just down the hall. So, I took the oxygen tank to their room, surviving the first major hurdle of the new job with what I thought was great success. This is when I learned as a hotelier you might be called upon at any time to do tasks for guests that I could not have possibly imagined actually being involved with when I turned in the job application.

The rest of the first evening was uneventful. I learned a lot of new phrases: city ledger, average daily rate, day rates, guaranteed reservation, and no-show, terms that all hoteliers know by heart. It was an interesting hotel with 114 rooms and three stories, just off of the main interstate highway, I-35. The room rate in 1985 for a single queen-size bed was $29.99. Doubles were $39.99 and the special truckers' rate was only $24.99 if you parked your big rig eighteen wheeler in the back parking lot.

We kept up with the hotel rooms sold using tiny rack cards (four inches by six inches) in a board about three feet across and two feet high behind the front desk. The room types were color-coded on the rack cards. A yellow card was a single room, a red card was a double room, a blue card was a king room, and an aqua card was a single waterbed room (yes, the hotel had waterbeds). When you looked at the board, if the room number was visible on the rack card, you could sell the room, as that meant it was clean and available. If the card showed "On Change," that indicated it was vacant and dirty, so you could not sell it until the head housekeeper flipped it over during the day. The folios we had with the guest registration information fit perfectly into those slots, so your board usually had a mix of open rooms, some

On Change rooms, and rooms with folios in them where guests were actually staying.

The other interesting aspect was the hotel had actual hard, regular room keys with a small yellow paddle attached to the key with the hotel room number engraved on the paddle. As I would find out later, we were supposed to change those keys and the guestroom locks out when a guest did not return their key at check-out. It is interesting to think about now, but in 1985, that was how room keys were handled and that was the level of guest security we had for our hotel rooms. The modern advances in key/hotel lock security were things we would have thought had come straight out of a "Star Trek" episode because they are so high tech now from those times in the 1980s.

For the job of night auditor, everything was hand-written paper-work. There was no computer. There was no real cash register, only a cash drawer. It was 100 percent paper with the audit itself being about thirteen pages. The real trick was each and every one of those pages interacted with the other pages, so if one page had incorrect information, it could mess up everything else. And I could not go home until it all balanced. That almost never happened, since I had eight hours to do the job and find the error. But it had driven me crazy on more than one occasion. I had gone deep into the night a couple of times chasing down a few pennies that caused everything to be off. I know all hoteliers can relate to that.

That first week went well. I learned a lot and my trainer gave me a reasonable overview of the operation or as much as he could, given he was again the part-time auditor who only worked on Friday and Saturday nights. He actually left me on my own after Wednesday of the first week because he thought I had the job down, plus he had to work Friday and Saturday and was not interested in working a straight, even though he was getting overtime. As I look back, I knew I had a basic grasp of it all, but the enormity of having the lives of every guest in my hands for those eight hours never really hit me until many years later when I was training new night auditors. I definitely stressed this part of the job to my team when I became a general manager. I thought the seriousness of that aspect had not been explained to me fully during that first week. You can learn something from everyone, even if it is not what they teach you directly.

Everything was moving along just fine: night audit, college, the hours, and the money. I was rolling along without any issues. I could actually complete the audit around 1:00 a.m. each night, then just work on my college homework until maybe 5:00 a.m. or so when I needed to make coffee for all of the truckers who were getting up that early to start their days. Long before the hotels that we are all familiar with now had the free breakfast similar to Denny's or IHOP, limited service hotels in 1985 had coffee, yes, just COFFEE for the guests. Breakfast offerings would change slightly as the industry moved into a new decade.

As I stated, everything was going fine until the beginning of November when I came to work on one Sunday evening to start my week, just like always. There was a new young lady working the 3:00 p.m. - 11:00 p.m. shift and a really tall guy with a dark thick mustache sitting in the lobby holding a clipboard, which I thought was definitely not normal. I walked to the front desk and told the new young lady I was Al, the night auditor. She told me her name and let me in from behind the desk. About that time, the tall guy got up from a chair in the lobby and walked in right behind me. Either I was about to get robbed by Bonnie and Clyde in some weird situation or something else was about to happen. The tall guy said, "So, you are Al, huh?" I said, "Yes." He then told me his name was Jon and he was the new "interim" manager. He needed to talk to me in the office. At this point, I am thinking okay, who is this new desk clerk and why is this Jon guy here? What has happened to my manager?

All the emotions start to fly around in the two minutes it takes for me to sit down in the office before he starts to tell me the story. The desk clerk is standing there as well, so now I am thinking, "Oh crap, am I about to get fired. What is happening?" Jon says he and the desk clerk are there from another hotel in the company, my manager is no longer there effective immediately, and they would be there for a few weeks, as there are some issues. He then proceeds to ask me about my job, how much I know about the night audit, and what my duties were each night. I tell him what I can handle and what I can do. He then tells the desk clerk she can go. He needs to spend some time with me. First thing he tells me is that he hears I am some math whiz and he wants my help locating some unusual activity in the books.

I did not feel that I was any sort of math whiz, but as I found out later, "math whiz" was literally written in my employment file by the manager who hired me because of what Lisa had told him during my original interview process. Funny how certain things like that stand out regardless of the truth or what I perceived to be true. It turns out over time, Jon would tell me I was a math whiz at reading hotel financial statements. It all seemed very easy to me, as apparently I could see the books in a different way than everyone else. Jon liked my thought process with the audit, the city ledger (the outstanding direct bill accounts), and ultimately the P and L (profit and loss statement) for the hotel.

As the story goes, my original manager who hired me had been fired along with the evening desk clerk, but no one ever explained why they were both let go at the same time. I honestly did not care because I was doing my job, going to college, and the hotel was not my first priority at the time. That was about to quickly change in the upcoming months, as Jon became one of my best friends, a great mentor to me in the hotel business, and ultimately my best man at my wedding a few years later. But, that first night really told the tale of where I could help him. He had me do a full report on all of the books, plus he wanted me to reconcile the hotel's checkbook, the cash, and all of the credit cards back from the past four months. Coincidentally this was about the time I had started the job, so I knew where to look for all of those items and it only took a few nights to completely reconcile it all. I had honestly not been performing these tasks for my job, as the previous manager did not have it on my list of duties. Moving forward, I was told I would be responsible for these additional tasks and it needed to match just like everything else on the audit each night.

Jon was a really great guy to learn from. He was living at the hotel while the company was working out the details of getting a new long-term manager hired. Jon would come down at least a couple nights each week to visit with me or teach me something new or just tell me about the hotel business. He had been in the business at that time for about ten years, so I thought he knew everything about the business, and I was a sponge absorbing everything he was telling me.

There was a scary incident that was certainly worthy of workers' comp, but it turned out I was more interested in doing the job than being off work or hurt. This happened on a regular Monday night just before Halloween and prior to my twentieth birthday, which was that Wednesday, October 30. I had just finished the audit around 1:30 a.m. and was making the final cash drop into the safe. The safe was an old one about two feet tall, but secured to the floor with a handle on the right side and a slot in the top about six inches front to back and maybe twelve inches across. The handle was designed for you to put the cash drop in the slot. Then you would turn the handle, the drop would fall into the safe, and only the manager could open it up during the next day to make the daily bank deposit.

There had been no previous issue with the safe. Just put the money in, turn the handle, and I was normally good to go. But, this night as I put the cash in, it got kinda stuck in the rotating mechanism and I could not get the handle to turn. The cash was stuck and no one would have been able to get to it, but I continued playing with it to try to figure out what was wrong. Of course, the smart thing was to put my left hand in the slot to attempt to free the envelope while I basically jammed the handle with my right hand to nudge the dang thing loose.

You can see it coming, and of course, it was going to turn out like you think it did. About the time I got one hand in the slot on top to free the envelope and hit the handle with my other hand, the envelope came loose when I pushed down on the handle. As the "roller" thing came around, it smashed the three fingers on my left hand still inside the top of the safe with a force I can only equate to putting your hand in a car door and slamming the door on it. Remember, I am completely alone, it is 1:30 a.m., the new interim manager, Jon, is upstairs asleep, and my hand is now bleeding all over the place behind the front desk. As I pull my hand out of the slot, two fingernails were essentially gone and the other is hanging by a thread. I could think of only one thing to do to stop the bleeding, so I ran to the ice machine, which was the old type where you opened up a big door and there was a plastic large scoop in there to get your ice out. Without thinking, I just rammed my hand right in there to see if that would help the pain and stop any of the bleeding. Nevertheless, I had just destroyed an entire ice machine full of ice with my blood literally ALL OVER THE ICE AND MACHINE.

It seemed to work, as the pain subsided after a few minutes. Then I had to find the first aid kit, which may or may not have been somewhere in the hotel's laundry room. Again, safety and security were not really part of the training process. I was in trouble, but I wasn't sure exactly how to handle the situation. Somehow, I found the first aid kit, figured out what to do with the remaining part of the fingernail, and held the bleeding in check. At no point did I call anyone else or think of anything other than it was my birthday week. I still had to go to school in a couple of hours. Then I had to go back to work the next night.

Filing for workers' comp or taking time off of work never occurred to me. I was taught: you work or you don't get paid, and I could not miss school or work. Jon came down around 6:00 a.m., saw the blood on the safe and the bandages on my fingers and asked, "What the hell happened?" I told him the story, to which he said, "You know no one could have gotten that money out. You should have just left it alone." I told him I obviously realized it just a little too late. He then said, "You're gonna be able to make it tonight, right?" That was old school thinking. No workers' comp and no going to the hospital, just would I be able to survive and make it to work and cover my shift. I did make it that next night. I somehow did survive that ordeal, and have the scars to prove it.

All this time, I was going to college as a finance major because my mother was a banker. I thought that was where the money was, so I needed to also be a banker. Plus, all of my childhood friends whose parents were bankers seemed to have money and big houses. I thought that was a good plan. I liked money and I certainly would like a big house someday. But that was all about to change.

As the next few weeks came and went, Jon was still there. But before Thanksgiving, he let me know that he was going back to his home hotel, which happened to be in Austin. Another manager had officially been hired. The new manager, Danny, was a younger guy, maybe twenty-seven or twenty-eight at the time. He seemed pretty nice and very knowledgeable about the hotel business, so I figured this would also work out. No reason to do anything different. Steady as she goes. I found out that Danny and the interim manager, Jon, had worked together for their previous company and they were buddies. That worked out because Danny immediately trusted me to help him with the paperwork while he wrapped his head around running the hotel, developing the staff, and making his mark with the company.

I would learn more about the company. It was based in Wisconsin and had originally been started by a man who was into real estate and understood the construction part of hotels. So in the early 1970s, he had started building his own hotels in the Midwest across multiple states. In the mid 1980s, he had set his sights on Texas. The hotel I worked at in Denton was the first of six that the company would end up building in the Lone Star State over the next few years. I mention this part because throughout my hotel career in subsequent years, I would end up working for another hotel company based in North Dakota and ultimately owned my own hotel with some partners in Wisconsin. Apparently, Texas was just my birthplace because all of my W-2s for my entire life seemed to come from up north.

With 1985 ending and moving into the early part of 1986, I was plugging away with college and the job. At this point, Danny was working hard trying to convince me I could make something of myself in the hotel business if I wanted to change my career path. I knew my mom would not like ANY change in the career direction that I was currently on, so I did not even think of approaching her with any of that talk. Sometime in late March, Danny told me that the regional manager from the corporate office was coming to town soon. He had put in a good word for me, so I should meet with him because there may be an opportunity to do something in the summer while I was out of school.

I thought, okay, it is worth the talk. I had no big plans at the time for summer, other than to keep working and maybe take a vacation. So what could it hurt to visit with the regional manager? I felt honored that Danny would think that highly of me. So it was all set to take place in April as school was about to end later that semester. I was curious about what they wanted, so we set up a lunch date to discuss it. That would become another day that changed my life forever, and it was only supposed to be lunch.

2

1986 – THE DECISION THAT CHANGED MY LIFE.

I was all set to go to lunch with Danny and the regional manager from the corporate office in Wisconsin. I had never had a meeting like this. There was not a true corporate type of environment at the movie theater I worked at in high school, so this was something completely new. I was now twenty years old and about to finish my sophomore year in college hoping to someday be a banker, following in my mother's footsteps. The lunch was set to take place at a restaurant close to the hotel on the north side of Denton. It was a quaint Italian place known for great lasagna. Apparently the regional manager liked to try new/local places. As I would learn more about him, he told me he hated chain restaurants and wanted the local flavor when he was on the road. When I was traveling later in my career, I liked the hole in the wall places too because every town has the chain restaurants. Not every town has that really good local restaurant with recipes passed down through multiple generations.

So, back to lunch. We met and the first thing Brett, the regional manager, says was, "I hear you are some sort of math whiz." I must have been the most famous math whiz in Denton, because it just kept coming around when I would meet new people from the company. Brett asked me what my plans were for the summer after school was out. I told him my plan was to work at the hotel, take a vacation, and get ready for my junior year of college. At this point, he said, "How about if you come to work for us and travel to our hotels in Texas. We need someone to help us where we may have a gap or need assistance while members of the leadership team from the different hotels go on their vacations." He told me I could still take my vacation and they would give me two weeks paid vacation even though I was not due for a week of paid vacation, much less two, until August. I would find out later they were hurting badly for support staff, as they were opening new hotels throughout Texas. They said I would be put on salary for the summer once I started in this "temporary role" and they would pay for any meals if I needed to stay overnight at one of the hotels or for an extended period of time.

This is where I learned what per diem was, and I thought I was really cool because I could "expense" food. I would also get to stay at hotels if I was on the road, and that sounded like a really exciting thing to be a part of. They told me I would be paid a salary of $1,200 a month for the summer and I would not have to clock in or clock out at any of the hotels. At the time, I was making $5.50 per hour, $220.00 a week, or $880.00 a month. They were giving me a "big" raise, I would be on salary, and there was no time card or time clock to worry about. I was all in. Let's get going! They explained that the general manager at the particular hotel where I would be assigned would set my schedule, but I was reporting to the regional manager for the summer. I asked, "Where do I sign and when do I start?" They told me I would start as soon as school was out for the summer. All they needed from me was for me to let them know my schedule and also to try to keep in the back of my mind when I wanted to take my summer vacation.

The offer was way more than I had expected, but now I had to prepare to tell my mom the plan. I knew she would not be on board at all. She was under the impression I was going to be a banker. My hotel job was not to affect my life or certainly my future. The talk with my mom was more engaging than I had thought. She was okay with it, AS LONG AS I WENT BACK TO SCHOOL THAT FALL. Well, that truly was the plan, and I had no thought of not continuing school. This job was just for extra money and to gain more business experience. Once I started back to school for my junior year, I would go back to my home hotel in Denton and continue on the plan I had in my head, no different than before my lunch meeting with Brett. My mom was somewhat supportive of this idea as well, so I was all set to finish school that semester and hit the road.

I was excited about this wonderful opportunity, but finals were coming up, so I had to stay focused and make sure I did not get too far ahead of myself. Over the next few weeks, Danny was giving me his insight and his ideas of what to expect as well as how to interact with the other managers at the hotels. The other hotels in Texas were located in Arlington, Mesquite, one near the DFW Airport, and one in Austin with another being built nearby. The Austin option intrigued me because I thought I would be able to spend some time with my friend Jon, who was down there running one of the hotels. When my sophomore year ended, Brett, the regional manager, had come down one more time in mid-May, and we had time to start planning my schedule. It appears the hotel in Arlington had the most need for help. The hotel had recently opened in early 1986. The summer was about to get extremely busy, and the hotel was located only a few blocks from the Six Flags Over Texas amusement park in Arlington. In the mid-1980s, Six Flags Over Texas was a prominent vacation destination.

Everything was all set. I was going to Arlington to work at that hotel the first week of summer. The plan was that I would drive there each day from my home in Denton. I would not stay over at the hotel because it was simply too busy. As you can imagine, they could not afford to have a room out of service for some kid to enjoy his time on the road in his new "fancy" job. I was a little disappointed because I really wanted to travel and stay at the hotel to use this new per diem benefit. The title they gave me for the new job was "operations manager." My role covered all aspects of the job, and none of the assistant managers at the hotels would feel I was there to do anything other than help. I was no threat to them or the staff. I would later learn the "threat" thing was real, and it could even be broken down into different departments at a hotel or the "you stay in your department and don't bother mine" type of mentality. This type of attitude is certainly not conducive to a team atmosphere, but it happened then and sadly it still happens to this day. At the first hotel in Arlington, it was not an issue, so I started with a good team from that standpoint to help me understand the business. I simply helped them out.

The manager at the hotel in Arlington, Gerri, was a smart young woman. This was her first manager position leading her own hotel. She was in her early thirties at the time and had studied hotel management while in college and working at a few large full-service hotels. She had a lot of experience, so I was excited to spend time with her and learn more from her even if it was scheduled to only be a few weeks. The hotel was definitely in need of help, as it was consistently filling all of its 114 rooms on a nightly basis once the summer travel season started. The hotel was built exactly the same way my home hotel was built. The front desk and the laundry room were the same, which was good for me because I knew where everything was the moment I arrived.

I was scheduled to get to the hotel on Monday morning, June 2 around 9:00 a.m. Brett, the regional manager, told me I would be there all day. It could be a long day, so there was no reason to get there too early. Brett just didn't want me to be late. There was no way I would be late. I arrived around 8:45 a.m. to meet with Gerri, the manager, to get started. We had a good talk to start the day. She explained what had been happening and where I could help. After maybe an hour and a half, a very nicely dressed woman came into the office, looked right at me, and said, you guessed it, "Is this the math whiz kid from Denton?" Gerri said, "Yes, this is Al. He is here to help." The lady said, "I heard you were coming. What do you know about housekeeping and the back of the house?" I told her I did not know much about it. She then told me her name was Imelda and she was the executive housekeeper for the hotel by DFW Airport. She was there to help out as well and she would teach me everything I would ever need to know about housekeeping. I thought, "Okay, whatever you think. I am here to assist anyone who needs me and if Gerri and Brett want me to learn housekeeping or be involved with Imelda, I will be happy to help."

I did think it was interesting that she was dressed nicely. I would learn very soon that type of dress was what she wore every day. I never saw her in the same dress twice. The other executive housekeepers I knew or would see at other hotels wore the same uniform as the staff, but not Imelda. She was amazing and the learning was going to start right away with her in Arlington. Gerri gave me my schedule for the next two weeks. It was desk shifts and no audits, but there were definitely weekend days. This whole "salary" situation was about to come into play because the schedule had me with one day off for the upcoming two weeks. The benefit was I did not have to clock in or clock out. But after calculating the hours I was about to work and the time of travel back and forth each day to Denton (about forty-five minutes each way), I was not really sure if I was even going to make the $5.50 per hour I was making working the basic night audit in Denton the past eight months.

No complaining. That was just how it was, and I had better suck it up because I had committed to at least doing it for the summer. Here we go. Throughout the course of the next two weeks, I would see Gerri occasionally. She was stuck back in housekeeping cleaning rooms and bringing down laundry. I thought it was strange to see Imelda running around the front desk more, but she was now my buddy. When I would work the morning shift, she knew I was stuck at the desk, so she would bring me a plate of food for lunch.

Apparently the housekeeping team did a potluck almost every day in the breakroom and they would make extra for whoever was on the front desk. Imelda also taught me a lot about what her job as executive housekeeper entailed and what actually was happening during the day. I had only been a night auditor working 11:00 p.m.–7:00 a.m. and never learned the day-to-day operations of the hotel. She was also the one I would credit with teaching me "hotel Spanish." That was what I called it because she wanted me to be able to communicate with the hotel housekeeping staff who were predominantly Spanish-speaking. She would constantly go over everything related to the hotel, and she would teach me the Spanish word for it all. This was a great lesson to figure out that you never know where the learning opportunity is going to come from. Never stop learning, never stop growing, and never stop encountering people or and interacting with people because they look different than you or even speak a different language.

I had picked up the first shift quickly and was helping Gerri with anything she needed. She figured out she did not want to be stuck doing housekeeping while I was hanging out working the front desk. After the first two weeks on the desk, she asked Brett if I could stay longer, as she was going to put me in housekeeping to work with the team. She would then cover the desk. To her, I was "free" labor because I was on the corporate office payroll and I could help with the back of the house. She had been trying to hire a front desk clerk. That person was coming on board, but she did not want to let me go to another hotel.

During the course of the next couple of weeks, I was working in housekeeping, either teaming up with one of the housekeepers stripping linen out of the rooms or doing laundry. I could fold towels like nobody's business, and at the time, all of the sheets were literally the same. We did not have fitted sheets, thank goodness, because when they finally arrived on the scene a few years later, I could never figure out how to fold them properly. Folding fitted sheets properly is definitely an art form, and for those of us in the industry who can do it, kudos to you. I commend your effort and hard work.

I enjoyed my time in Arlington. It was a great learning experience, but it was time for me to go on vacation by the middle of July. A friend of mine and I planned our trip, and we headed out for two weeks of rest and relaxation on a beach. It was a great time, and we certainly had a chance to discuss what was happening with my career. He felt I should pursue a career in hotels as much as I could. Honestly, I was ready to see what my next assignment was and which hotel they would send me to.

As it turned out, my next opportunity would come in the form of working at their hotel in Mesquite, Texas. It wasn't really Mesquite. It was more like East Dallas, but right on the border of the two cities. So for the sake of where it was located, let's just go with Mesquite. I got back from my vacation on Saturday, had Sunday off, and was supposed to report to the hotel first thing on Monday morning. I was refreshed, ready to see what was happening with the hotel, and ready to get started.

I got to the hotel. Again there was a young woman who was the general manager. Her name was Jan. She was as smart as Gerri from Arlington, but she had no interest in me working on the front desk or in housekeeping. Jan wanted me to go right into maintenance. I guess Brett had told her that he wanted me to learn that department. Plus the hotel was slow at the time and I could gain some knowledge from the maintenance man before the hotel got busy in the fall.

I started right away in the maintenance department the next day. This time, I was allowed to stay at the hotel while I was working there. I went home that first night and loaded up my car for a two- week stint in Mesquite. This trip and assignment turned out to be a great experience. The maintenance man was bilingual, in English and Spanish. I asked him to speak to me in Spanish as much as possible so I could learn more Spanish. He was a terrific teacher of their maintenance programs, and working with him was fun. On the weekend, I just hung out with the front desk clerks at the hotel and helped where I could. Constant learning was the name of the game. That was something my parents had told me—keep learning and keep growing—and even in this microcosm of my hotel career, I really took that to heart. Working with the maintenance man for that short stint was just as valuable to me as if I was spending time with Jan, the general manager. If you can learn something new every day, you will never stop growing.

As my time in Mesquite wrapped up, Brett called and asked if I could go to Austin for a couple of weeks, as they were just about to open their second hotel in the city and they needed an extra body. That way, I could hang with my buddy Jon who had been in Denton previously. This would be great. I was going to stay at his hotel on the north side of Austin and spend time learning more of the management concepts from him in between doing punch lists and working long hours at the yet to open new hotel on the south side of Austin.

What I did not know at the time was the reason they wanted me in Austin. It was for Jon to get a sense of where my head was related to the company and my returning to college, which was now definitely on the horizon. In other words, I needed to make a decision. I had to decide whether to go back to school or start my hotel career with the company. I knew what my mother thought and what she wanted me to do (go back to college—no question about it), but I was starting to enjoy the hotel business. I felt I was good at it and each day I was getting a better understanding of how to run a successful hotel. Honestly, I was starting to think, "Gosh, I think I could really turn this into something beyond going back to school and becoming a banker."

I arrived in Austin, and even though I had been there before to visit my high school friends who were attending the University of Texas, my two weeks there this time with Jon really gave me a sense of the city. In 1986, it was eye opening with its famous Sixth Street, the University of Texas, the miles of running trails along Town Lake, and the world-class restaurants. It was an awesome experience. Jon and I had a wonderful time just visiting and it was fun to just be with, learn from, and hang out with my buddy. This was probably the time that we became close friends, and I still cannot thank him enough for his insight and wisdom into the hotel business and the multitude of things I would learn from him over the years to come.

As I was about to wrap up my time in Austin, Brett happened to fly in to visit with all of us. It was great to see him in person, as I had been traveling all summer and really had not seen him since he gave me the new "job" working at other hotels. I knew he was there to see everyone, both hotels, and both GMs; however, he was also there to see me to find out where my head was about going back to college. Jon had told him that he thought I might be wavering on going back to school and they should not let me get away if I wanted to continue to follow the current path in my hotel career. The lesson here was that you might have a plan or an idea of what you want to do, but circumstances change and you never know what idea or plan someone else may have for you. You must always be open and available for the different options that cross your path.

We all went to dinner the first night when Brett was in Austin. It was a joyous occasion, as the new hotel was about to open in the next couple of weeks. Everyone was excited at what would now be the sixth hotel for the company, with the possible idea there would be a total of twenty hotels built in Texas sometime over the upcoming years.

During dinner, Brett asked if I had time to visit with him the next day. Of course, I said yes, and we met that next morning at 10:00 a.m. in the breakfast room of the hotel. Earlier in the year, we had met for lunch, which had redirected my life. Now we are about to meet for breakfast, and this time, it was really going to change my life in a way that I could have never imagined. He started out by saying how glad he was that I had accepted the breakfast opportunity, and everyone really enjoyed working with me during the summer. He asked me when I had to return to school. I said I needed to get everything lined up in the next week, as my classes would fill up quickly. Time was of the essence to get it taken care of and paid for to make sure I started the school year on time.

This is when it all happened. It was around 10:20 a.m. on August 11, 1986 in Austin, which happened to coincide with my one-year anniversary starting at the hotel in Denton. I can see that moment in my head vividly just like it is happening right now. He said, "Well, we would like to make you an offer to stay with us and not go back to college. What do you think?" I said, "Well, my mom will kill me because this is NOT the plan we have laid out, but tell me more about your thought process." He went on to say that they had not yet hired an assistant manager at the hotel in Mesquite. The guy I had met while I was there earlier in the summer had left. They were looking for someone to replace him and everyone agreed it should be me. I was obviously very flattered, and as our discussion continued, he told me that I would never have to punch in for the rest of my career once I got into hotel management, I would be a salaried employee with untold future opportunities from their company, and they wanted me to say yes.

I told him I truly could not answer him right then. I needed to discuss the decision with my mom. I was scheduled to travel back home in a few days, so I wanted him to give me time to visit with her. I would get back with him right after that if he was okay with the timeline. He agreed and said to get back with him right away once I spoke to her. He then told me the salary for the assistant general manager position at the hotel in Mesquite. I would also have to move to Mesquite, so they were going to give me a "signing bonus" of $1,500 to help move anything I needed from Denton and pay my deposit on my new apartment or just to use to purchase stuff I needed for my new place. This was probably also a bonus for helping out all summer and I thought it was great! Again, I was a poor kid from Denton and was being offered $1,500 to play with if I accepted that amazing opportunity. I am thinking, "Okay, I really do like the hotel business."

Since I still officially lived at home, there wasn't really anything to move, but I would need to rent some furniture and get some basic household items. So this "signing bonus" thing was going to be a big help if I decided to take the job. All the planning would have to wait because I was now about to drive back home in a couple of days, then somehow convince my biggest fan (my mom), but also the most logical, thoughtful person in my life, that I was thinking of not going back to college. The lesson I was learning and was about to come to understand was that no matter what direction you think you are going, life is an ever-moving target and you cannot ever close yourself off to opportunities that come up, even if they seem completely foreign or scare you to death.

Brett gave me the week off once I got home to meet with my mom to make my decision. I then needed to get back with him the following Friday one way or another. The original plan had been for me to go back to the Denton hotel in some capacity while I continued going to school after the summer. The company had kept their word and there was a spot for me at the hotel. So I could go back. But I had now convinced myself that I wanted to go on this new path and accept the position as assistant general manager in Mesquite. Next up, I had the discussion with my mom and had to convince her the opportunity would be the best thing for me over returning to college.

It was now the moment of truth. Would she be supportive or blow a gasket, concerned that I was throwing away what I had started in college and banking/finance was still the way to go, no matter what some regional manager had told me or offered me. The conversation started easily enough over dinner at our house. Then I dropped the news on her. She took it all in for a while as I was describing what their plans for me were and what they were wanting me to do rather than going back to college. I knew she was skeptical, but to my surprise and almost unreal shock, she said if I wanted to do it, she would support the idea, but only for that year. She said, "You tell them you will take this year off from college, but if anything goes wrong or things are not moving in the direction you want, you will have to pull back to finish college."

My mother was right of course, so on that Friday, I called Brett to tell him what she said, what I was thinking, and ultimately that I would accept the job and forego college for that year. He said he was excited for me. He understood how important college was to me, but the offer was a great, once-in-a-lifetime opportunity for me and as a twenty-year-old young man, they had the ultimate confidence in me. Then, he dropped a little nugget that would come to mean something in the future, but did not register at the time. He said, "Go to Mesquite, learn as much as you can, as fast as you can, and you never know what could happen next. Tell your mom we will take good care of you." Well, he was right. Time would reveal the truth because what would happen in early 1987 made all the other moments possible from that point forward. I had officially accepted a position as the assistant general manager at the hotel in Mesquite, Texas.

Later that Friday afternoon, I spoke with the GM, Jan, at the Mesquite hotel. She told me how excited she was that I was going to be her new AGM and we were going to make a great team. She asked if I could come down and start the following Wednesday, which worked out just fine. So we were all set. Everything was lining up. I started working with her and absorbing as much information as possible. She was a great teacher, and even though we were somewhat close in age (I was twenty, soon turning twenty-one), she was either twenty-seven or twenty-eight with an incredible eye for detail at the hotel. My lessons learned from her were that nothing should be left to chance and people are always looking at everything you do. Many times, I have thought about how those lessons were incredibly important as my career moved forward in different positions. For her to impart that knowledge on some young kid like me was truly a blessing.

I enjoyed working with her. We sold out the hotel for the first time ever on the weekend of the Texas/Oklahoma Red River rivalry football game in October during the Texas State Fair, which was held at Fair Park only a few miles down the road in east Dallas. This was exciting because surprisingly enough, that hotel had never had a sold-out night and the team was really pumped about finally accomplishing that feat. We stayed busy for the rest of the time during the fair. Shortly after that, Jan told me that she was leaving the company and a new guy was coming to be the GM of the hotel.

This was honestly somewhat surprising news because I thought she loved working at the hotel and loved the company. But she was originally from a different state and wanted to go back home to be closer to her family. The lesson I was learning was that not everything stays the same and people you work with today or have in your life today may not be there tomorrow. Their path is not going to be the same path as yours. I was very sad to see her leave. She was an awesome mentor. The moment she left was the last time I ever saw her, but her impact on me was certainly memorable.

As we were cruising along to finish the year, the new general manager arrived. He was also young, maybe twenty-five or twenty-six at that time. His name was Ricky. He was from one of our hotels up north, but had wanted to move to Texas and this was his opportunity. He was incredibly intelligent and very driven. He had previously been in the military, starting right out of high school and had finished college after his time in the service. Once he got his degree, he began his career in the hotel business with our company. I was excited to work with him, as he was closer to my age than any of the other GMs and was also a college graduate. So maybe he could give me some insight into my decision to forego college and go along this path in the hotel industry for the year.

He and I got along great. I was working a lot, much more than I had been with the previous GM. I worked some double shifts and most weekends, but I think what Ricky was trying to express to me was that the hotel business is truly twenty-four hours a day, seven days a week. If you are the AGM, manager on duty, or GM, you may have to work a lot. So you had better be prepared for anything to happen, and most of the time at that hotel it did. To clarify what a double shift is on the front desk, most hotels run three shifts. They are: 7:00 a.m.–3:00 p.m., 3:00 p.m.–11:00 p.m., and 11:00 p.m.–7:00 a.m. At many hotels, if you are the front desk clerk, you may be the only person on the shift. Regardless of the day of the week, it may just be you. So, when you work a double, think of working sixteen hours straight, starting with one of those shifts, but finishing with another one. Most of the time, it seemed I got stuck working 7:00 a.m.–11:00 p.m. That is a long day to be sure. Most of the time, you don't plan on it, but someone calls in sick and you are the only one there. So tag, you are it, unless you can get someone else to come in and cover for you.

Something that never happened to me during my hotel career, but it did happen to other people was someone having to work a triple shift. So think of starting to work on one of the shifts and you are working straight through until that same time the following day, with no rest and no sleep. You cannot leave the desk. You are "it" for twenty-four hours straight. I can only imagine what a terrible feeling that is when it happens, but you may not have a choice. I often wondered when that happened if the employee who caused it felt badly for the person who was stuck at the hotel or if they were indifferent because the person working was usually a manager, thus getting paid their salary. Just a random thought only a true hotelier would understand.

That "someone calls in sick" stuff seemed to happen to us a lot as we were finishing out 1986. It ended up being me who covered those shifts up to the point that I was working double shifts almost as much as I was working single shifts. I can remember vividly once working a double and there was a new 3:00 p.m.–11:00 p.m. desk clerk I was training. Around 8:00 p.m., she came to the office, which was just behind the front desk, and I was dead asleep with my head on my desk, just slumped over from exhaustion. She woke me up with her question, which I answered and apologized profusely for falling asleep. I was terrified I could get fired, so I decided to come back early the next day to tell Ricky what had happened before he heard about it. He had been working a lot of hours too, so I had hoped he would understand. As I came in to talk to him and tell him, he could tell I was upset, so we actually left the hotel to go to breakfast together. We discussed the whole thing. He said he was not mad, he understood, and said it would get better, but I just had to hang in there and make sure the staff did not see me fall asleep again.

I was thankful we were growing our relationship and building something at the hotel together. After that discussion, I never fell asleep again working the desk, no matter how tired I would get. I just had to stay awake and suck it up. That would be put to the test early the following year, but by then there was a much bigger goal ahead, so I could "suck it up" even if it was an awful situation. The lesson of this whole episode was that the people around you rely on you when you are the leader and no matter the circumstances, you still have to portray leadership. If you are put in charge, you need to be in charge.

One more story that came up to finish out 1986 happened in early December. I was not at the hotel when it happened, but would get there shortly thereafter, and it still resonates with me to this day. I had worked the night audit shift and had gone home after my shift ended at 7:00 a.m. to rest a little bit before coming back to the hotel for my regular AGM shift, which started at 2:00 p.m. I had barely gone to sleep when the phone rang at my apartment and somehow I was able to be coherent and answer the phone. It was probably around 11:00 a.m. and it was Ricky, the GM, on the phone damn near frantic, saying that I had to come back to the hotel right away. Our front desk clerk had just been robbed.

This meant she had been robbed in broad daylight at 11:00 a.m. I quickly put on some clothes and headed to the hotel, which was about ten minutes away. As I got there, the police were everywhere and the poor desk clerk was clearly shaken up pretty badly. It was the first time I had dealt with a robbery at a hotel, which I always found to be amazing because there was never very much cash onsite. Most of the transactions were made through credit cards. Remember, there was certainly no internet or online purchases at the time. There was maybe $200 total in cash in the drawer or available to the desk clerks, not much more because you would make your drop into the dreaded safe that almost took my fingers off, as previously mentioned.

The worst part of this story was not the money taken from the hotel. That could clearly be replaced. It was again maybe $100 cash that the robber had gotten away with. The problem was the desk clerk had just gotten engaged to her fiancée. The robber saw her beautiful engagement ring and pointed the gun at her, demanding the ring. On top of being scared to death and in shock, she had now lost something of real value to her, not the hotel. It was an awful thing. I knew how much it affected her because even though she did stay with us and continued working at the hotel, she was never the same while she continued working with us. She ultimately claimed the ring on her insurance, which somehow came through and replaced it or matched the price of it.

From then on, the poor desk clerk was less engaging with people and was always leery of our guests, which made it difficult for everyone involved. I think I realized that in some weird way, her life would never be the same. I know I vividly remember the whole situation, and I was not even at the hotel when it happened. I am sure it must still cross her mind at times. What that taught me was no day is routine and as much as we are there to take care of guests and serve customers, some people may have other reasons to be in your hotel or your place of business. That day put a dent in my trust of people and let me know I should be careful and not let my guard down because we truly did not know who might walk in that front door at any time, day or night.

3

1987 – BECOMING A GENERAL MANAGER

As 1986 rolled into 1987, I had just turned twenty-one the past October. The hotel I was working at in Mesquite was doing well. All was right with the world and with my new career. At least that is what I thought. But, in only a couple of months, my life would change again forever. Ricky and I were getting along well, we had stabilized the staff, the hotel was getting busier, and I had planned on being there at least through the spring. But, of course, the hotel business always has a different plan and unforeseen surprises. This new plan was going to take me out of Mesquite and transfer me over to another one of their hotels.

Right after the year started, we heard Brett was coming down to visit with us, which was great news. He and I had stayed in touch periodically. We began to get close when he had come to visit as Jan was leaving and Ricky was arriving on the scene only a few months prior. Brett arrived, we saw each other briefly, and he said he wanted me to join him and Ricky for dinner the next evening. He also wanted to meet with me before dinner privately at 5:00 p.m. that next day. I was not worried, but I thought, "Oh, geez, is something happening to

Ricky because I sure hope not. I like working with him and the last thing I need is to have another change at the hotel now that we have it really moving in a great direction."

As the next twenty-four hours passed, I prepared to meet with Brett at 5:00 p.m., then hopefully enjoy a celebratory dinner because I sure hoped I was not going to get bad news. By now, he and I had built a good rapport with each other, and I thought he was impressed with my work ethic and my determination. I sat down in the meeting room and we chatted and talked it up a little bit. Then he told me the reason for the meeting. He said I had been doing an excellent job, so good in fact, they were moving me from the Mesquite hotel to the hotel by DFW Airport as the AGM starting immediately.

Apparently, the hotel by the airport had been struggling, so they wanted me to assist the GM and see what I could do to help stabilize the front desk. They would buy out my apartment lease and give me a $500.00 bonus to help move anything I needed to have relocated. They told me they wanted me to move back home to Denton and commute to the DFW hotel. They would also give me a gasoline allowance each month to help with the cost of the travel back and forth. Okay, that sounds great. I can live at home basically for free. They are paying my car's gas bill. I can pocket that $500.00 bonus. Let's go celebrate at dinner.

And celebrate we did. Unbeknown to me, all of the GMs in the DFW area had been invited to dinner. Gerri, from Arlington, who I worked with the previous summer was there, Ricky was of course there, and also the GM from the DFW Airport hotel was there. So we could catch up and maybe brainstorm for a bit about what his thoughts were concerning me coming over. That GM from DFW, Thomas, and I had met before when he had come over to the Mesquite hotel in the prior few months. I did not know him that well, but I was about to go to work for him, and it was good to spend some time with him for the evening during dinner.

For the first time ever, I had champagne as Brett looked at this as a promotion for me, even though it was a lateral move in my mind. Also, the new GM from the hotel in Denton was there, as Danny had left the company in the prior few months. Now I had to get everything set to leave my apartment in Mesquite and let my mom know I was coming home. Brett told me to get it all set and be at the DFW hotel on Monday the week after next, which was about ten days away. I made it all happen as planned. My mom was excited that I was coming home. The next step in my career was off and running at the DFW Airport hotel.

It was now mid-January 1987. The moment I got to the DFW hotel, I realized it was a total mess. There were employee issues, there were guest issues, there was one mess after another, and no one appeared to truly be in charge. Even though I liked Thomas, he was different from all of the other GMs I had worked for. He was not a leader, was not involved, and seemed to be delegating a lot of responsibilities to me. Oh, and weekends were just not his thing. He was not going to work on the weekends, and that was that. This was a bigger hotel than the other ones I had worked. There were more things to deal with. This is also when I learned what a "distressed passenger" was in hotel lingo. A distressed passenger was an airline passenger who had been displaced by the airlines due to a canceled flight, and now they needed a place to spend the night before they could take their new flight the following morning. They were given a voucher and told the voucher would get them a hotel room. The hotel would take care of them. Of course, I now know what a voucher is, but back then in early 1987 it was all new to me. The airline gate agent would call the hotel, tell the hotel they needed X amount of rooms, and mention the people were on their way to the hotel. The bus showed up and all of these people were in the lobby!

I had been so happy at the Mesquite hotel over the prior few months. We had built a great staff, but now I had somehow walked into a living hell where nothing was going like it was supposed to and Thomas was hands off. The staff was trying to keep their heads above water. What a mess! One of my first encounters with the weekday morning clerk was when I came in early for my evening shift. As I walked in, her husband was behind the front desk with her. They were smoking cigarettes together like they were at home just shooting the breeze. I walked into Thomas' office, asked if that was okay, and if he was going to say anything to them. He told me, "She is really good, don't worry about it. We have bigger fish to fry than worrying about her and her husband smoking behind the front desk." I was thinking, "You are the GM. This is your hotel. This is your deal, but this might be the problem. No rules. No standards. Now I am starting to under-stand why there are issues all over the place."

But, there was one good part of this chaos: that was Imelda, the ex-ecutive housekeeper at the hotel. She was the woman who wore a dif-ferent dress every day who I had worked with briefly at the Arlington hotel the previous summer. She was glad to see me and told the staff all about me. She of course told everyone I was the "whiz kid" from Denton who she had taught how to do housekeeping when I was help-ing her in Arlington. I told her I had been working on my Spanish in Mesquite and asked if she would help me continue to learn more when I worked during the day with her. She said of course, so more learning was coming my way. It is good to always keep learning and keep growing no matter how bad your current circumstances may be. You can do something for yourself even in the worst of times.

I ended up working almost every day from the time I arrived at the hotel. A day off was nowhere on the horizon. And that was never more apparent than what happened one weekend only a couple of weeks into me being there. We could not establish the staff even though there seemed to be plenty of applications coming in (the late 1980s recession was on the horizon and people were looking for jobs). Thomas was not following up and hiring anyone. It was driving me crazy because the applications were piling up on his desk and he would not let me contact the applicants to bring them in or schedule them for interviews, much less hire someone to support us or start to fill in all of the shifts I was stuck covering. I think he felt, "I have Al here to cover these shifts, and I can save payroll, so let Al do it and my payroll costs will be low." That is all well and good, but he was burning me out and I knew we were getting worse by the day, ugh!

I was scheduled to work the night audit shift for the upcoming weekend, which was fine. I could handle it and it might allow me to actually get some sleep during the day, since the idea was no one would bother me, knowing I had been stuck working the 11:00 p.m.–7:00a.m. shift. Plus being in Denton might give me a "buffer" with the company, knowing I was about thirty minutes away from the hotel. That all sounded good in theory, but of course it was all about to go sideways in the craziest way possible. On that Friday, I took the "day off" to rest and catch up before driving out to the hotel around 10:00 p.m. so I would be on time and maybe catch up with the 3:00 p.m.–11:00 p.m. desk clerk for a bit.

The plan went like it was supposed to and the evening appeared as if it was going to be reasonably quiet. Nothing too big was coming and we were at about seventy percent occupancy. I wasn't tired during the night and finished the paperwork around 3:00 a.m., so I was just waiting for the newspaper guy to show up. Back in 1987, as a night auditor that was a big deal. You would see an actual human being around 4 a.m. bring in the newspaper, so you had something to read and/or do prior to the guests starting to stir, usually around 5:00 a.m. at that hotel.

There was a breakfast hostess who would arrive around 5:30 a.m. Really all she did was to make sure the coffee was fresh, there was some orange juice available, and the donuts that were delivered looked good for the guests. That was it. There was nothing more than coffee, orange juice, and donuts available for guests at our hotels. Think about how many breakfast items are now available at every type of hotel, regardless of how small or how big. Most hotels have what amounts to Denny's or IHOP available during breakfast for their guests and many times it is FREE. Boy, how times have changed over the years I have been in the business.

Back to that weekend in question, my shift was supposed to end at 7:00 a.m. I was then going to head home to rest before having to do it all over again at 11:00 p.m. that Saturday night. No biggie. I had been there, done that many times previously in Mesquite, so it should have been a good day. But, as many hoteliers can attest, that 6:45 a.m. call to the hotel from the first shift clerk who is supposed to start at 7:00 a.m. is NEVER a good thing. In this case, it was not going to turn out to be a good day.

Sure enough on this Saturday morning, the phone rings right at 6:45 a.m. It is the first shift clerk who is supposed to be there at 7:00 a.m. telling me her car will not start. She cannot make it in on time, but she would update me as she started getting the situation resolved. Okay, that is not so bad. I can stay for a little while. Even though it was not what I was expecting, I could deal with it because I was not tired. Plus I could spend time with my friend, Imelda. She was scheduled to work that Saturday in question and would be there around 7:30 a.m. The GM never worked weekends, so I knew he was not coming to the hotel on that Saturday. Back then, there were no cell phones, only pagers, which were a new technology, and of course there was the proverbial answering machine at a person's home. At that time that morning, I thought there was no reason to bug him. He probably wasn't going to answer anyway and me staying over a little bit wasn't a big deal.

Imelda arrived at 7:30 a.m. right on time and of course she asked me why I was there. I was not supposed to be there when she got to work. I was supposed to be home sleeping by then. I caught her up on what had happened. Then she told me that the front desk clerk had pulled this stunt a couple of months ago before I arrived on the property as the AGM and the front desk clerk might not show up at all.

Well, this is just great news. I may have to be stuck at the hotel until 3:00 p.m. to work a dreaded double shift. I am not happy about this part at all. Imelda said, "Thomas knows the front desk clerk is not very good, but she has been showing up regularly for the last few weeks and he doesn't want to address this with her because he might have to actually discipline her, or worse." So, I prepared myself for the inevitable double shift. Around 9:00 a.m., I decided to call my mom and let her know I was still stuck at the hotel. I didn't want her to worry. I was hoping to be home soon. I would keep her updated.

Around 10:00 a.m., I have not heard a word from the front desk clerk. I decided to call her and see if she answered. Was she coming in or was she not? I called. Of course, she did not answer. The call went to her answering machine. I left a message which was very nice, but I also gave her my concern that I had not heard from her. If she could please touch base with me, I would really appreciate it. Around noon, Imelda came down and brought me lunch because the hotel had the same type of arrangement as the other hotels. The staff shared a pot-luck lunch or meal every day.

I do not know if hotel staff members still do this, but I always had a great respect for the ones that did and on this day, I really appreciated them being there to help me out. I was stuck on the front desk with no escape in sight until the next front desk shift started at 3:00 p.m. Imelda asked me how I was doing. I told her I was hanging in there, but I was more frustrated than tired at that point. She said if I had not heard from the missing in action front desk clerk by 1:00 p.m., I should call Thomas and let him know. At least he would have an update on what was happening at the hotel.

So, at 1 p.m., there was no word from the front desk clerk. I decided I would call Thomas and leave him a message explaining what had happened. I also paged him, but I did not expect a call back, which was fine. He was starting to worry me that he did not care, so this issue was going to be up to me to deal with. Around 2:00 p.m., the front desk clerk called me to tell me that the car was still not working, but she would be there the next morning (Sunday), so not to worry. She told me "not to worry" after I had been at the hotel for fifteen straight hours. Of course, you are thinking the same thing I was at that point. Even in early 1987, if your car won't start, why would you not just get someone else to take you to work or simply get a taxi? There may have been no Uber or Lyft back then, but there were certainly taxi cabs, especially around the airport area. Heck, I would have even paid for her to get a taxi to bring her to work and at least relieve me from being stuck at the hotel since 11:00 p.m. the night before.

Then to my surprise, just after her call, Thomas called me at maybe 2:30 p.m. He said he "had been out" so he was sorry he missed my call. This of course did not explain why he did not respond to me paging him. I guess I could live with the first part of him being out and not getting back with me, but it was disappointing for him to wait that long to touch base with me, given that I had paged him. It could have been the front desk clerk needing him. He did not know, but it did not matter. He was on the phone with me then.

I gave him the update on what had happened. I told him I would of course finish the shift and leave at 3:00 p.m. when the next desk clerk hopefully showed up. But, if the morning desk clerk's car did not start on the next morning, he needed to be ready to help me out if possible so I did not have to work another double shift. He said no problem. He would be home all day the next day (Sunday). If something went wrong, he would come in to relieve me so I did not have to work another double shift for the second day in a row.

The 3:00 p.m. front desk clerk did show up. I just needed to get out of there and go home. I was now tired and ready to hit the bed. I told the front desk clerk I would see her in eight hours, as my next shift would start at 11:00 p.m. I got home quickly. My mom asked me what had happened. I gave her the brief overview. I explained it was the hotel business. I had done this double shift thing before when I lived in Mesquite, so it was no big deal, not to worry. She said what I was describing did not happen in the banking world. As that semester was going to end, she was still thinking I should go back to college in the fall. She may have been right at the time, but I was too tired to deal with that. I needed to get to bed because my next shift was going to start in just a few hours.

I woke up that evening with no problem. I ate and I hit the road to get back to the hotel to work the night audit shift. I got there and the front desk clerk gave me the rundown on what was happening. It should be another quiet night, so I was not expecting any surprises through the shift. But now, the bigger question was would the first shift front desk clerk show up the next morning or would her car still be broken, preventing her from coming to work. We would see. Well, I had to wait all night, but right on the button at 6:45 a.m. the phone rand and it was her. OF COURSE it was her and OF COURSE the car issue had raised its ugly head. So she could not make it to work on time, but she would try her best to get there.

At that point, I started giving this grown woman the options to get to work, even if it was not within my authority. I told her to call a taxi, and I was even willing to pay for it because she needed to come to work. She said she would check with her husband and call me back. Wait! You have a husband who may have another car, but you are saying you cannot come to work because you are having trouble with your car. This was not adding up, and I was getting more frustrated by the minute. She hung up. I was again stuck at the hotel with no prospects of getting loose from the desk anytime soon.

Imelda was not scheduled to work that day, but even on her days off, she would call in to speak with her assistant. Just after 8:00 a.m., she called and sounded surprised to hear my voice, but probably not all that surprised because she had warned me about this. She had no faith in Thomas, as he was no longer leading the hotel in any meaningful way. She asked if I needed anything. I told her I was okay. She reassured me the housekeepers would get me lunch and take care of me if I was still there at lunch time. I then put her through to speak to the assistant, who came down right away to tell me they had made fajitas for lunch and had plenty for me if I was there at lunch time. This conversation was almost entirely in Spanish, because her English was getting better and my Spanish was getting better. That part of my learning was really starting to grow and I really loved it.

As the morning continued on, I knew I was going to reach out to Thomas. At 10:00 a.m., I called him. He did not answer and I left a message on his answering machine. Lunch came and went with no word from the desk clerk and no word from Thomas. But I had a great lunch courtesy of the housekeeping team. Their fajitas were absolutely delicious. I really started to love working with the back of the house team and had a great deal of respect for them. They were terrific people and I had a real appreciation for how hard they worked and cared for the people around them.

Around 2:00 p.m., as the shift was scheduled to end, of course I heard back from the desk clerk. I had now been there again for fifteen hours straight for the second day in a row. She proceeded to tell me she had not been able to work out the details of getting to the hotel. By that time, I simply did not care and told her I covered it for her, no problem. I essentially hung up on her. I'd had my fill of her and her ridiculous excuses. I was tired by that point in the afternoon and wanted to get out of there for the day. I needed some sleep. Then to top off my day, Thomas finally called back around 2:30 p.m.

You are probably wondering if Thomas and the desk clerk were in cahoots because they called me at exactly the same time the day before. They were not coordinating their calls. They both knew by calling that late, I was bound to just stick it out and finish the shift. Thomas proceeded to tell me he overslept. I am thinking, "For gosh sakes, it is 2:30 p.m. Where the heck did you go last night? Plus how late did you stay up to sleep in for that long?" I had been up since 9:00 p.m. the night before and I was still stuck at the damn hotel Thomas was running into the ground.

I told Thomas the desk clerk's story. He said he would deal with it. I did not believe him, but I was going home in a few minutes. I wanted him to get off the phone at that point. He then added a sweet nugget. He told me I could take off on Monday, since I had to work two doubles that weekend. Ya think? I had just put in thirty-two hours in the past forty hours of real time, and he was going to be generous and tell me I could take a day off. The situation had now become a real problem for me.

That episode ended. By Tuesday, when I came back to work, everyone knew what had happened because Thomas told Ricky, the Mesquite GM, who then told other GMs. It was a small, growing company where gossip spread quickly even without the internet, social media, or cell phones. I think what had really happened was Thomas had spoken to Ricky. They were friends. Thomas was done with working at the hotel, but had not previously known how badly he did not want to be there any longer.

Within three weeks of that whole situation, Thomas had resigned and was on his way out. That was fine. He was barely showing up anyway and I was now almost running the hotel by myself. All of that was okay with me, as well as the rest of the team. The best part was coming. Jon from Austin was now coming back to take over the DFW hotel. I was excited to be working with him again. We were going to kick butt and take names. I knew he would not put up with any shenanigans. It was great news. Well, it was supposed to be great news. But that of course was about to change at the end of February. I just did not know it yet.

By that time, there was a new regional manager in place, David, who had previously run a few hotels for the company. He was a good guy and pretty straightforward. But I did not know him as well as the previous regional manager, Brett, who had given me that first opportunity. I was working too hard to worry about who was at that level. My job had been going one hundred miles per hour at the DFW hotel. I was just trying to survive until Jon arrived from Austin to right the ship and get us back on track. He was scheduled to arrive on March 1. We had not gotten a chance to talk very much. He had simply told me he was excited to come back to the DFW area. I was giving him updates on the hotel, but nothing too detailed. I was going to wait to give him all of the scoop when he arrived. The day of his arrival would not overlap me with him as my GM. Once more my life was about to change, this time forever!

Leading up to Jon arriving from Austin and taking over, David had spent a lot of time at the hotel. We were working together quite a bit trying to get us back on track quickly. That was good because even in that brief time, we were learning a lot about each other. Plus it was giving him an up-close opportunity to see if I knew what I was doing as an AGM. Leading up to March 1, when Jon was set to arrive, Brett, the old regional manager, was coming back to town. He had been promoted to regional manager/vice president, which meant David reported to him in the hierarchy of the company.

I came to work on Wednesday, February 25. David told me that Brett was looking for me and I needed to call him right away. I thought, well, it was out of the ordinary, but I figured it was a good thing, so here we go. I called him. We spoke for a bit, then he told me he was coming to town, and for me to be in Denton that Friday. We needed to do lunch, and I was not to tell anyone else. I didn't think too much of it at the time. As you can now imagine, when I went to lunch or dinner with him, it was usually something big, or at least that was my impression. I felt that this time would be no different. It turned out to be the lunch that would change my life and honestly the lives of many other people from that moment forward.

David told me that he knew I was doing lunch in Denton that Friday and again, I was not to tell anyone. I could have the day off. He told me to just take it easy that morning and get ready for lunch. That sounded fine. I presumed he would know about it, so no big deal. Here we go for lunch on Friday, February 27, 1987. I arrived a little early and waited for Brett at the front of the restaurant, which was near downtown Denton by the square.

As I write this, I realize how quickly all of it was happening to me. My first "real" meeting with anyone from the corporate office had only been a year before that lunch with Brett. My world had been moving from different hotels, in different cities, with different people, and certainly different experiences. I had not even been keeping track of how quickly my life was spinning. What I did not realize at the time was all of these experiences had been designed to prepare me for that lunch and that moment with Brett. The restaurant was small, but had great

Texas home style food. I figured he may have never been there before. Plus it was usually pretty quiet.

As I sat there on the porch of the restaurant waiting, I saw a car pull up and it had four people in it, not just the one I was expecting. Out of the car popped Brett, David, Jon, and a guy who I had never seen before. They were all laughing as they were walking up. They all greeted me. I said hello to the new guy. He introduced himself as Dan. Then we all sat down for lunch. Brett started the discussion by saying how incredibly proud he was of me, how much everyone in the company liked me, and how impressed they all were with me.

Okay, great, very flattering, but what is happening and why are you ALL here in Denton to meet with me? I was thinking I was meeting with only Brett for lunch. But, as you may have learned by now, these meetings always turned out well, and now this one was no different. He told me that he had the chance of a lifetime for me and that he needed an answer by the following Monday. I would have the weekend to decide. He wanted to offer me the position of general manger at the hotel in Denton effective immediately.

Yep there it was. They were offering me, the twenty-one-year-old whiz kid from Denton, Texas, the chance to be a general manager of my very own hotel, which would make me the youngest GM in the history of their company! They believed in me so much they wanted me to start right away. But, and this is the big hurdle, I would have to give up going back to college. This was a life- and career-changing situation and there was no going back from this point. Take the job and give up college, or stay at the hotel as AGM with Jon as my GM and then go back to school that fall. That was honestly the idea all along, or at least according to my mother's plan.

During lunch, we discussed at length all of my training and development over the past year, who I had met, what I had learned, all of the departments I worked in, and the comments and ratings of me from everyone who worked with me over that time. I had been on a crash course of management training for the past year since I left college at the end of May 1986. Of course, I did not know any of this, as it had not even dawned on me what they had planned all along. That plan was of course to help at the hotels, but also to throw me right into the fire at each of those different properties. I had been working with different people, different scenarios, and certainly different personalities that I would possibly have to deal with as a real leader, or in this case, general manager, of my own hotel.

As we wrapped up lunch, they let me know that earlier that morning the GM of the hotel in Denton had been fired and the new guy I was meeting, Dan, was going to be the acting/interim GM with me. Whether I took the job or not, he would stay until they found someone to fill the position. I told them I would give them my answer by that Saturday morning after speaking with my mother. This time, I was sure she would say no. School first, no shenanigans of being a GM at twenty-one. What did I know and how could I possibly handle this responsibility?

That Friday evening, I went to dinner with my mom and gave her the scenario. To my great surprise, she damn near teared up and told me that this would be an amazing opportunity. If they believed in me that much, I should accept the offer, and because of my knowledge of the Denton community and her connections, I would do great. She told me to go for it. The risk would be in not taking it and regretting missing the opportunity to chase a dream. At that moment, I realized I had made her very proud of me. School may have been the destination, but this journey was going to be even greater. Do not let it get away. I guess that is what parents do. You expect them to go one direction and they surprise you by going in another direction.

I knew I could do the job or I would die trying. There was no quit in me, and I believed so strongly that I could run my own hotel at twenty-one, I did not have to wait until the following morning to reach out to Brett. I actually called him that evening after dinner and said, "Yes, I am in. I am happy to accept the position of general manager of the hotel in Denton. Let's get started." He was glad to hear back from me and said for me to come to the DFW hotel on Monday. I could sign the paperwork with everyone involved. I was the general manager of the hotel effective Sunday, March 1, 1987. Wow—what an amazing feeling!

I went to the DFW hotel on that Monday morning to sign everything, say goodbye to the staff, and spend time with Jon, who was now the GM of the DFW hotel. The best-laid plans had fizzled of us working together, as I was about to take the reins of my very own hotel. He said he would help me however he could, but he knew I could do it since the first time we met in late 1985. I just had to believe I could do it. They had been hoping I would give up school since, from their perspective, hotel management was in my blood. I gave him the rundown on his new hotel and what it needed. We went to lunch and I drove off to MY hotel in Denton to start as general manager. I did come back a few times over the following couple of weeks when they needed some insight into something that was happening. But they clearly had it under control, so my focus then turned to my own hotel.

As I pulled up to my hotel in Denton that Monday morning, I realized it had only been about eighteen months since I had started my career at that hotel. Now I was back running the place. This is a memory I still look back on fondly. To think I had turned from a teenager into a young man and into a grown-up in that short time. I already loved the hotel business so much. Dan, the interim GM, was there. We caught up and started right in on it. He was staying at the hotel. We did not stop working or going over things that first night until well after midnight. I was a sponge and wanted to know everything about the hotel. That went on for the next few days at a blistering pace. He was great to have with me, as he guided me on the stuff I may not have seen. But there was no stopping my learning.

The staff was taking to me well, even though as I look back on that time, I was so incredibly young. I am thankful for their patience because I must have appeared to be a teenager who daddy had just given the keys to the car. My job was not to run it into the ditch, fingers crossed. After about a month, Dan was going to head back to his home hotel up north. I was apparently ready to fly solo once and for all.

All of the GMs in the DFW area had decided we would go out for a celebration and to say goodbye to Dan before he left. We decided to go to Billy Bob's Texas in Fort Worth to hear Gordon Lightfoot in concert. I had never been to Billy Bob's before, even though I would go many more times in the coming years. That evening was going to be my first venture into the famous Fort Worth Stockyards. Also, I had bought a new car in the prior few months. It was a black used 1983 Mustang GT. Dan and I were going to take it to Fort Worth. We set out that evening with me driving, although I would not be driving back. I was literally flying down the highway from Denton to Fort Worth (about thirty miles in driving distance) doing about ninety miles per hour with no care for traffic or worry about the highway patrol. I loved that little car, and we were enjoying the ride together.

I was not a big drinker and never had been. Plus, with my crazy schedule, I never knew when I would have to work a shift or have to fill in. Drinking was just not an interest of mine. But, that night at Billy Bob's with my friends and feeling my oats, I was enjoying some adult beverages. There was an actual "breathalyzer" coin-operated game at Billy Bob's. Before we left, we decided we were all going to get our alcohol level tested before hitting the road. It was maybe fifty cents, so we each grabbed two quarters and started in on it. I waited my turn, grabbed the straw, and blew into the machine. Back then, I probably weighed about 150 pounds, so I was a pretty skinny kid. As I blew into the breathalyzer, my blood alcohol level came back as 0.22, more than TWICE the legal limit, which was 0.10.

Well, apparently, I had quite a few drinks that evening and was clearly in no condition to drive. I gave the keys to my Mustang GT to Dan and we headed home north to Denton. I had told my mom I might stay at the hotel, so for her not to worry about me coming home that evening. As we drove home, Dan was clocking the car at about one hundred miles per hour. To say it is a miracle we didn't get a ticket or worse is an understatement. We were too fast, too dumb, and too out of control to be on the road, for sure.

We got to the hotel and Dan told me, "You CANNOT go through the front door of the hotel. You are too drunk and your staff CANNOT see you like this. Let me get you a room key and you go in the side door." At that moment, I realized he was right. I was not just some kid hanging out with his buddies any longer. I now had real responsibilities and me acting like the cool kid was not acceptable. I was the general manager, the hotel was MY baby, and the staff was MY team and they would respect me. In that moment, or maybe more to the point, when I woke up the next morning in the hotel room with the worst hangover you can imagine, I knew that was it. I would NEVER be in that position again and no one would EVER have to drive me home again. The lesson was about how people can be affected by your actions or actually by how your actions are viewed or perceived by others. It may mean everything. You never know who is watching you.

I do not know if I have ever told that story to anyone because I was so embarrassed or just thought what in the world was wrong with me. The company and those people had given me that incredible opportunity, and I was being an idiot with it just to hang with the cool kids. Thus, to this day I will not drink to excess and many of the people around me have not even seen me with one drink, much less drinking to the level that would jeopardize them, my job/position, or even my life. As the saying goes, "With great power comes great responsibility." For me, my responsibility was to never let anyone around me down because of my lack of maturity.

The spring of 1987 was fading into the summer. The hotel was doing well. We had a really good staff that had been built by Dan, and I was constantly working to improve the team. The previous GM, who had been fired, had simply let the place go. So for me to clean it up was not too difficult. I put in a lot of long hours and weekends, and we were on our path to recovery. I was incredibly happy to have accepted the job. The team believed in me and I believed in them. However, there was one employee who was just not getting with the program. He was the weekend evening clerk, so his shift was 3:00 p.m.–11:00 p.m. He was coming in late, not finishing his paperwork for the shift, and the other clerks who worked the weekend were having issues with him. I had spoken to him about it, as I was there most weekends, and I would see him coming in late. I had addressed it with writing him up, but it was not getting any better. I was about to fire my first employee as a GM.

You can imagine, with me being the GM at twenty-one, most of my team was older than me, except for a couple of the desk clerks who were college kids at the University of North Texas. The employee we were having issues with was a lot older than me (maybe in his mid-thirties) and had a "real" job during the week. Our hotel was his part-time weekend job. I had called Jon, the GM at the DFW hotel and told him about the situation. He said to run it by David, the regional manager. Jon did say that type of behavior could not continue and I was probably going to have to fire the guy. I think I knew that, but every once in a while having a peer who gives you some positive feedback about your thoughts is not a bad idea.

I did speak with David right away. He asked if I had followed all of the protocol regarding write-ups. I said yes, then I faxed him the write-ups. Fax machines had literally just come on the scene, and they were fed with thermal paper. I sent the write-ups over. He called me back, said the paperwork looked good, and I had his blessing to fire the front desk clerk. Back then, there was no human resources person at our corporate office. We were making decisions in the field. That system had always seemed to work out fine. Well, at least we thought everything was working out fine in our naïve way of thinking back then. I told David I would take care of the situation that upcoming Saturday at 3:00 p.m., I knew what to do, and I would page him afterward to let him know it was done.

When the front desk clerk came in, I was there just like most Saturdays. But this time, I was in my suit and tie. That was a little different, but of course he was late, which certainly was no different. He walked in. I asked him to come back to my office. He came in and as I closed the door behind him, he said, "You're going to fire me, aren't you?" I said, "Well, we have discussed this previously in your write-ups. You are still coming in late and you are still not finishing your paperwork. So what do you think I should do if you won't correct this situation?"

He told me with a straight face, "I knew that you would probably fire me, but I did not think you would have the guts to do it since you are just a kid. What do you know about running a hotel at twenty-one? Does your dad own the company or something?" At that point, I told him he was being terminated for excessive tardiness and failure to complete his shift paperwork as assigned for his position. He almost looked shocked as the words came out of my mouth. Everything I said was professional and directly on point. I opened the door. He walked out and that was over. I had now fired my first employee as a GM.

The entire situation changed my perception about how the employees were viewing me. But I was so proud of myself for facing it head-on and not flinching when he was trying to intimidate me or call me out for my age. I paged David, the regional manager, and he called me right back. I told him what happened. He said it was a good lesson to learn from a couple of different perspectives. First, people may view you differently because of your age, but stay professional and never waiver in doing the right thing. Second, if you are EVER not sure about what to do in a situation, always follow the rules and you will never go wrong. I took that to heart and to this day, I am very appreciative of him telling me that advice because he was 100 percent correct.

As the year went on into the latter part of the summer of 1987, I was about to get my first chance to go to the corporate office for the biannual GM meetings in Madison, Wisconsin. I knew all of my GM friends from Texas would be there. Even though I had flown many times, this time I felt I was going as a professional businessman. This was going to be an adventure. Funny, back then, it seemed you could basically bring anything on an airplane as a carry-on item and check as many bags as you wanted. There was no extra cost or extra expense. The corporate office coordinated our travel plans, and we were all going to fly from DFW to St. Louis then to Madison. All of us from the DFW area were on the same flight. I was dressed in a suit and a tie and I carried my toiletry items in my briefcase. I was trying to be so cool and big-time.

We got to Madison later that afternoon. The whole week was great. We had meetings, some training, a tour of the city and its famous State Street, a visit to the State Capitol building, a boat ride around Lake Mendota, and a golf tournament coordinated by one of the other regional managers who was based out of the corporate office. During the week, I met the owner of the company, some of his family, and all of the corporate office team. I felt so at home with all of them. They were truly genuine people and the culture they had created was something I desired to be a part of for a long time.

Somewhere in between all of the happenings was when I decided the hotel business would be my career and my life. I was not going back to college. How could I give up the hotel business? I truly cared for those people and I was in love with the hotel business. I made lifelong friends on that first trip who I continue to stay in touch with to this day and will for the rest of my life. That trip wrapped up. We came back home, and I was completely reinvigorated with even more determination and passion than ever to make my little hotel in Denton, Texas, into something great.

Moving through the fall of 1987, everything was on pace. I was putting together a good team at the hotel, I was learning a lot from everyone around me, and I was truly loving my life at that point. One good thing that was starting to come into play was my involvement, or maybe participation, with the Chamber of Commerce and the Convention and Visitors Bureau (CVB). Both of the leaders of these entities were fairly new in their positions, with them only being there a couple of years at that point. However, they would each play a significant role in my life over the next few years and beyond.

I started to figure out that even though I was not going back to college or might never be a banker, there were a lot of bankers involved in the Chamber of Commerce. My mom knew most of them and told me to connect with them if possible because I would never know what door they might be able to open for me next. Through my mom and those experiences with the Chamber of Commerce, I was learning the power of networking and connections in the real world. To me, it meant everything and I was building a "family" with the people of my hometown. The lesson was to NEVER underestimate the circle around you and the people you meet. They all might play a role somehow or someway in your life. Everyone you come in contact with could be your next employee, next boss, next business partner, or just a trusted confidant. It is your job to determine how to give them value so they want to be a part of your life. Giving is so much more rewarding than taking!

4

1988 – LEARNING HOW TO REALLY MANAGE AND GROW IN THE HOTEL BUSINESS.

As 1988 started, I had begun to put a good staff in place at the hotel. I was learning, they were learning, and we were growing together. We had also started to design new ways to look at staffing. I was running a full-time staff on the front desk Monday through Friday, but created a rotating schedule on the weekends, implementing an "A" scheduled team and a "B" scheduled team. What I had learned by trial and error was that many of the weekend part-time employees liked the idea of having extra money, but they did not like having to work every weekend at the hotel on top of working their full-time job during the week. So, I came up with the idea of one weekend the "A" team would be on for their three shifts and the following weekend the "B" team would be on for their three shifts. I was running nine desk clerks rather than the usual six that all of our other hotels were staffing. I then added a tenth desk clerk who was a floater just to fill in when someone called in sick or to help out when needed. He was a college kid who one of the front desk clerks knew and recommended. He was dependable.

Staffing might seem like it is obvious, but at the time, those shifts and the way they were viewed were pretty static. In those days, you had the regular schedule. Why would you change it? It had been done that way forever, just leave it alone. As a twenty-two-year-old kid, I knew what we liked at our hotel because we were working together for the greater good. Even though I was the GM, it was our hotel. The best part was for the entire year of 1988, I did not have to cover a single shift. We had full coverage in our budget, 168 hours a week, which was obviously twenty-four/seven. But after the debacle I had dealt with at the DFW hotel in early 1987 as an AGM, I would not repeat that situation. I truly felt my team would never let me down. The lesson I had learned was to be innovative and sometimes think outside the box, but include your team or the people around you, as they may view something from a completely different perspective than you do.

Our housekeeping staff at the hotel was predominantly Spanish-speaking, and I loved working with them. They were great to be around. We had instituted the potluck meal where everyone would bring food and the entire team would share. This was what we had done at the other hotels in the Dallas area, so now we did it at my hotel. On Fridays, I would buy fajitas because it was what they wanted. I bought the whole staff the big meal one day each week. I was still living at home, and I seemed to have money to burn, so spending it on the staff made me happy. Those lunches were a great time for us to bond, as I would have lunch with them on Fridays and we would all speak Spanish together. However, this seemed to drive Hanna, the executive housekeeper crazy. Hanna did not speak Spanish. My fluency was getting better and better by the day. I was not trying to undercut her, but her days were numbered because of her terrible attitude. That was going to be my next big task to tackle.

It was sometime in early February 1988. I came out of the office and was headed to the laundry room down the hall to check in with the staff. As I was walking toward the laundry room, all I could hear was Hanna yelling. I was thinking, "What the heck is the problem?" Her voice was getting louder and louder as I got closer. It did not appear to me that she was angry, just talking REALLY loudly. As I got to the guestroom, I walked in. She was there with one of the housekeepers and still talking loudly. I saw the housekeeper, who was relatively new to the hotel. She was kinda shuddering near the bed. I knew that housekeeper did not speak English. Hanna was speaking in English. LOUDLY. I asked Hanna, "What is the issue? What is wrong? Hanna said, "Well, I am trying to tell her that her bathrooms are not getting cleaned very well and she is going slower than the other housekeepers." I said, "Well, it looks like you have scared her half to death. You do realize she cannot understand a word you are saying because she only speaks Spanish." After I said that, Hanna just looked at me like I was an idiot.

I told Hanna to leave the housekeeper alone and to come to my office so we can figure out what the issue is and get beyond this situation. I then told the housekeeper in Spanish to relax, take a quick break, and come back to the room to finish her work. Everything was going to be okay. When we got to my office, Hanna was mad. She was a Caucasian woman in her late fifties who had been at the hotel for a couple of years. We were just not seeing eye to eye on the direction of the hotel. As we began our conversation, I asked her why she thought yelling was going to get her message across to someone who did not speak the same language. She said, "They understand what I am saying. They just choose to not listen and I am tired of it." I said, "That may be true, but rather than raising your voice, maybe try to speak in a regular tone, which may help calm down the situation." She said, "That is stupid. You have to make sure they know you are in charge and respect your authority."

I had learned in that quick exchange Hanna was not going to be my executive housekeeper moving forward. She understood the language barrier. Instead of thinking the staff was deaf and talking loudly, she was completely disrespecting them and was going to make sure they were either intimidated by her or scared of her. I told her to please tone it down. We had a good staff around us and we would have to work together if she was going to thrive in her position. She then told me, "I have got this. You don't know enough about housekeeping to deal with it. Just leave it up to me." I was not sure what to make of that, but our conversation was done. As she left, I knew I was about to make my second call to David to ask permission to fire someone.

I picked up the phone immediately, called him, and told him the story. He said he knew her from when the previous GM was there. He said he was surprised I had kept Hanna that long because there had been some issues with her very similar to that situation. He asked if I had any write-ups on her or any other documentation. I said, "No, not really." Well, that was enough for him to say, "You cannot fire her, but you can certainly write her up for insubordination for the way she talked to you." I said I would take care of it the following day. He told me to send the write-up over so he could approve it. So there I was using that stupid thermal paper fax machine again, but it was what we had. So it was what I did. I sent the write-up over to him.

The following day, after the write-up was approved, I saw Hanna arrive. I let her get the team off and running for the day, then I asked her to come to my office. She strutted in like she was something tough and with the "what do you want?" look on her face. As she sat down, I went over the events of the previous day. I said it was unacceptable behavior on multiple fronts, including the treatment of the staff. But ultimately, the big issue was her insubordination toward me.

Well, I thought she was loud the previous day. She completely blew up at me, giving me the riot act of how I did not know anything and I had no idea what was going on in housekeeping. She felt it was HER department and she had done all of the work back there long before I arrived. There were a few more choice words involved, but at that point, she got up and said she wasn't going to deal with the situation or take anything from some dumb kid who had no idea how to deal with the real world. And with that, she got up, stormed out, and quit!

That whole encounter was a unique lesson. I was learning how some people do think they can intimidate someone else or have the other person fear them, rather than respect them or try to work together. At that moment, I made a promise to myself that I would never do that to any of my team, no matter where or when. I did not want anyone to actually be afraid of me. Respect was one thing, but ruling by fear and intimidation was not the way I wanted to be viewed or lead my team. To this day, that lesson still resonates with me! The other lesson is someone who speaks a second language or more than one language, regardless of the accent, should be viewed as a person who desires to learn. Maybe you could learn from them.

Another story that impacted me greatly happened in August 1988. At the hotel, check-out time was 12:00 noon. On one particular day, there was a room that still had the deadbolt on the door. The "Do Not Disturb" sign hung on the outside and the guest inside was not answering the phone. The new executive housekeeper who I had promoted after the fiasco with the previous one came up to me and said, "Hey, something is wrong with room #111. We cannot get the guest to respond." I told her to get Geoff, the maintenance guy on the walkie talkie and tell him to meet me at the room. We would figure it out. Geoff came down, and I told him the story. At that time, the room deadbolts could be turned from the outside with a small key we kept at the front desk. I had grabbed the little key in case we needed to access the room.

Geoff was an interesting character in his own right. I had hired him at the end of 1987 after our other guy quit. Geoff was a Vietnam vet and may have had some slight PTSD. Back then, a lot of those issues had not been fully diagnosed. He was a nice man, very gentle, had a lot of knowledge, and could fix anything. So we got along great. He liked the housekeeping staff and they liked him. So when we had to deal with any issues, the housekeeping staff respected him enough to reach out. He did not speak Spanish, but they had a great rapport with him. He was their buddy who took care of the problems in the rooms so they did not have to.

As I knocked on the guestroom door, there was no answer. Geoff told me to give him the little key. He would get us in. I said, "No, I got it. Let me do it since I am here." I opened up the door, continuing to knock as we walked in. On the bed was the guest, a gentleman probably in his mid-fifties to early sixties. All I could see was blood splattered on the back of the headboard. There was not much else left to describe. He was dressed in his clothes from the evening before: nice dark slacks and a blue button-down shirt. His body was propped up with a couple of pillows behind him. I did see the gun laying on the left side of the floor where it must have fallen afterward. I immediately told Geoff, "Don't touch anything. Close the door behind us and do not let anyone in there until the police arrive." He had a weird look on this face. I got the sense in that moment he may have seen a dead body before. All I knew was we had to leave and not touch anything.

It may be obvious I had never seen this before, but in an instant I knew what it was and what to do. I'm not sure how I knew, since this was not in the general manager training manual. Geoff and I both left the room. I told him, "Just stay there. Don't move from the spot outside the door, and don't say anything to anyone." I ran down to the front desk to call 911, which was actually a new thing back then, as it had just started to be implemented into the mainstream of police departments in the United States. It seemed like Denton had just started with the 911 program. At least that is what I remember.

I told Jenna, the front desk clerk what was happening and hoped she didn't panic. She seemed okay, but maybe slightly unnerved. I went into my office to call 911. I told them the story. They said they would be on the way and told me not to touch anything or do anything. The police officers arrived. There were two cars and three officers. I walked them down to the room. Geoff was there. We all entered the room. The officers asked who had been in the room. I said just Geoff and me. A couple of the officers stayed in the room. I walked out to the hall-way with the third one. That officer began asking me more questions related to when the guest checked in, what his name was, if we had any form of ID on him from the registration card, how he paid, that sort of stuff. I answered all of his questions, with the help of Jenna, the desk clerk, who had his registration card. She again seemed unnerved, but got through it. Thank goodness, she kept her wits about her.

In about thirty minutes, a hearse from the funeral home pulled up into the hotel's back parking lot. The police had called them. They were there to take the body and start the process of notifying next of kin. By now, the housekeeping staff knew what was happening. I was trying to console them and determine if they were okay. Again, there is no manual for this type of situation with so many people involved after the fact. They took the gentleman's body out in a very quiet man-ner through the back entrance. It was very surreal to know that man had taken his life in our hotel.

I told the housekeeping staff to come to the front desk after the authorities left. I had a brief meeting behind the desk with the entire team. A couple of them were really shaken up. I told them they could leave for the day if they wanted to. We would take care of only the stayover rooms and get those cleaned. We all said a quick prayer. Two of them did decide to go home: the housekeeper whose room it was and her sister, another housekeeper, who she rode to work with that day. Everyone was hugging each other as we broke up the meeting. That day has never left me, even after all of these years.

I have often wondered what was going on in that gentleman's life in that moment that he had to make such a terrible choice. In subsequent days and weeks, the desk clerks who had seen him during those few days he stayed at the hotel would discuss the situation with me. Often, the discussions related to whether we could have done something or said something that might have had an impact on him to change the direction he took. I am not sure if we could have done anything to prevent his death, but from that moment on, I decided to never take anything for granted. I learned that in an instant, someone can make a decision that has a profound impact on others around them. If anyone reaches out to you or you see an issue, it never hurts to connect. You may be the one person they need in that moment, or they could be dealing with something you may not see or even know about. Kindness can go a long way in someone's life—always be kind!

After that day, the staff was convinced we had an extra "guest" at the hotel. They were certain we had a ghost and that room was haunted. We referred to the ghost as "Stanley." A few of the staff even said they had heard strange noises from that hallway or near the room, even when it was not occupied. I only had one weird encounter about a year later. I had purchased a brand new car, so it should have had no issues, or at least that is what I thought. I don't remember what happened, but I was having a rough day and was frustrated. I said something to the effect "Stanley" was cursing the hotel or something just completely off the cuff, with no real intent or direction. I was simply upset. Karin, the evening front desk clerk said, "You'd better cut that out. 'Stanley' is going to hear you and he will not be happy." Karin was talking like he was a real person. I remembered she did say she had heard things when she was alone late at night, but she had made peace with him and I had better take it easy.

I didn't really listen to her, but as I was leaving to get into my brand new car, the damn thing would not start—would not start as in there was nothing, no tick-tick-tick like it was trying to start, and no power anywhere. I turned the key and it just was not happening. So, I came back in to call a buddy of mine to come and give me a jump or get ahold of Karin's brother-in-law, who happened to be a mechanic. As I walked in, Karin was looking at me, and with me not even saying a word, she says, "Something is wrong with your new fancy car, isn't it?" I said, "The stupid thing won't start." She said, "That is impossible, it is brand new. You pissed off 'Stanley.' I told you to be nice. Look what you did."

I called my friend. He wasn't home. Karin told me her brother-in-law was out with friends. So I was stuck until I could get ahold of someone. She offered to give me her car to get something to eat, as it was getting later in the evening. But I told her, "I am fine. We will figure it out." She said, "Just tell 'Stanley' that you are sorry and he will give you your car back." I was still skeptical, but she looked to be every bit as serious as if someone had literally hijacked my car. If I wanted it back, I had better make amends with "Stanley." As the situation entered the end of its first hour with no relief in sight, I kept going out to the car, with nothing working at all.

By the time we got to the second hour, I finally relented. While I was sitting in my office, I said, "'Stanley,' please give me my car back. I am sorry." Karin told me that should have done it and my car would probably work then. Of course, I am thinking, "Yeah, right, whatever." But, I kept those thoughts to myself because I didn't want "Stanley" to hear me. I plopped my butt down in the driver's seat and inserted the key. I could see Karin looking out the window at me, giving me the thumbs up sign. As I turned the key, all of the power came on, the ignition kicked in, and the car started right away, with no issues at all. I saw her clapping in the window and giving me two thumbs up at that point. I left the car running, rolled down the driver's side window, and went back inside the hotel. She calmly told me, "Told you to be nice to Stanley." I was never a doubter again in the power of being positive. Never speak badly about or get frustrated with anything you simply don't understand.

As 1988 wrapped up and we approached 1989, I was having a wonderful time being a general manager. My life was hitting on all cylinders and I truly loved everything about the hotel business. I knew I had made the right choice and the hotel business would be my career path for the rest of my life. But 1989 was about to have a few surprises in store for me that would help expand my learning curve exponentially.

5

1989 – EVERYTHING IS GOING GREAT. YOU ARE SENDING ME WHERE?

My hotel was doing great, we were hitting our budget goals every month, and I was participating more and more with the Denton Chamber of Commerce. I was also getting involved with the little hotel association we had created in Denton. That part would come to play a very big role in my life many years later. But at that point, I just thought it was cool to be a part of a community of fellow hoteliers.

Before I get into where I would end up spending my summer, I had an unusually strange encounter one late night in mid-May 1989 that most hoteliers can relate to. It was odd, amusing, and interestingly sad all at the same time. We had such a great staff that I rarely had to work the overnight audit shift. But one of our part-time front desk clerks called in sick late on a Friday afternoon for their overnight shift. No one on the team could cover it, so it was mine to work. No biggie. I went home, took a nap, had some dinner, and was ready to go to work overnight. The hotel was slightly busy, but not too busy. I actually thought I could finish my paperwork I had put off or organize my office. I would finish the audit around 1:00 a.m. Then I would be alone and it would be quiet. That was the plan, as my shift was going to start at 11:00 p.m. I was actually excited to work it.

Our swimming pool at the hotel in Denton was outside of the building on the back side next to the back parking lot surrounded by a wooden fence with a single gate entrance. The pool was open from 7:00 a.m.–11:00 p.m. Usually the first shift clerk would open it each morning and the evening desk clerk would close it down doing their last rounds before their shift ended. This particular night, Karin, the evening desk clerk told me she had not yet locked the pool, as it had been a little busy. But she could go out and do it if I wanted her to. I said, "Don't worry about it." At that moment, I thought no one would be out there that late anyway and it would give me a reason to walk around the hotel to see the outside at night.

I did not think about dealing with the pool for a couple of hours. But after I finished the audit, I needed a break. I thought that was a good time to go lock the pool down plus take a walk around the building. At 1 :00 a.m., it was usually very quiet, so no problem. I got the flashlight and the keys and I was on my way to the swimming pool. I did not notice anything out of the ordinary. But as I got closer to the area, I realized there were people in the pool. Now I am thinking, "Ugh, I will have to kick them out. What in the world are they doing out here this late?"

As my steps got closer, my awareness grew much keener. As I got about fifteen feet away from the swimming pool gate, I realized why these two people were in the swimming pool at 1:00 a.m. They were heavily involved romantically with each other in our pool. Again, many hoteliers may be able to relate because this could have happened to any of them. But, at that moment while it is occurring, you are confronted with the issue of dealing with it or letting it go, presuming they will leave at some point. I did think in those terms, as well. But I just needed to get them out of there. I was going to make a noise with the keys or shine the flashlight up against the building. Maybe they would see the light and get out of the pool.

None of those tricks worked. Then I was at the pool's gate about to open it up. As I walked into the pool area, they saw me and they finally stopped what they were doing. I told them, "I am very sorry, but we have to close the pool for safety reasons this late at night and you need to go up to your room." Without missing a beat, the woman got out of the pool minus her bathing suit and walked up to me. Either she was going to slap me in the face or she was drunk and unsure of what was happening. Nope, neither one of those was the answer. She came right up to me and said, "Well, Sweetie, you are welcome to join us. We can all have a really good time. No one will ever know." The thought never crossed my mind to accept the invitation. So in short order, I told her, "No, thank you. My job is to keep the hotel safe. I am very sorry, but the two of you will have to leave." The man never moved. I didn't really even look his way. I walked away from her and presumed they would leave after I headed back in.

About fifteen minutes later, I heard the back door of the hotel open. I saw them walk in with their towels covering themselves. The man never looked up and I never looked over. All was right for the night. The evening finished up, I wrapped up the shift, and just chalked that one up to crazy stories. But it was about to get crazier. That morning, I was honestly not thinking of telling anyone. Just let it go and keep the secret. Well, that was the plan. No reason to bother anyone with that story. By the time the first shift front desk clerk came in at 7:00 a.m., I was feeling pretty rested. So I decided I was going to stay and spend the morning with the team.

Remember, I am from Denton. So growing up there, I knew a lot of people in the community. Around 10:00 a.m., I was behind the front desk when around the corner from the elevator was the woman herself from the previous night's encounter at the swimming pool. About thirty seconds after she walked out, the man appeared. Even though I didn't recognize her, she noticed me right away because I was dressed exactly the same as I was when I first encountered the two of them at one o'clock in the morning.

The woman said something to the effect, "Fancy seeing you here." As the man walked up to check out, I recognized him immediately. At the pool, I really had not looked at him, since she was the one confronting me in all of her glory. He was a well-respected businessman in Denton and the woman was NOT his wife because I knew his wife. He looked at me. I looked at him. Neither of us said a word. They walked away. The front desk clerk asked me if I knew them. I immediately said, "No." From that moment to writing this book, I had never told that story. Even though I saw the man and his actual wife many more times over the years, I was in such an awkward position, I did not say a word. I never saw him or the other woman at my hotel again.

In late May 1989, David, my regional manager, came to the hotel for his regular visit. But that time, he had a different reason for the visit. I did not know it until we went to lunch. These regional guys loved taking me to lunch and dropping bombshells and another one was coming. He told me that everything was going well at our hotel. He was very happy with me and proud of what I had built. He then proceeded to tell me that one of the hotels in the Midwest was in transition, the GM had left, and they were thin with backup help going into the summer. They wanted me to go up there to run the place.

I asked if he meant all summer, as in how long and more specifically where. He said they were searching for a GM, but it might take a couple of weeks. They were needing help right then. Even after the new GM was hired, they were going to send that person to another property for at least a month or so to train and learn the systems, which meant I might be at the hotel all summer. I asked what was going to happen to my hotel and who would be running it. He said my team was doing so well, they could handle it on their own. He told me my scheduling system of ten desk clerks added such an enormous amount of flexibility, he felt good about me leaving. He would come to the hotel to do payroll every other week. If they needed anything, he would help or they could call in resources from the other hotels from the metroplex.

One more thing that was important of course was which hotel I was going to be at all summer. He then dropped the bomb on me that the hotel was in Rockford, Illinois. I thought, "Where in the world is Rockford, Illinois, and what am I going to do there for three months?" I quickly figured out where it was, about ninety miles west of Chicago, ninety-five miles from Milwaukee, and maybe seventy miles from Madison, Wisconsin. Okay, this is sounding good because by that time in 1989, I knew all of the GMs in the Midwest. I was going to go up there, get the hotel settled down, and hang with my buddies on the weekends. The company had hotels in each of those cities. In fact, we had multiple hotels in each of those cities. So I was thinking I would spend each weekend with my friends in one of those cities. It was going to be GREAT!!!

I broke the news to my staff that I was going to be gone for a while. They were sad, but very excited for me to take that trip and spend my summer in Rockford, Illinois. I then started making calls to my friends up there and we began right out of the gate to make plans to get together for weekends and baseball games at the Milwaukee Brewers and Chicago Cubs. Plus my friends were telling me about all of the festivals in each city. It was going to be a once-in-a-lifetime opportunity, so let's get going. My flight was set up to be one-way, since the company did not know when I was coming back. I flew into Chicago O'Hare. One of the other GMs picked me up to take me to the hotel in Rockford. The hotel had made a deal with a rental car company. So I got a car that next morning and I was all set.

For any of the hoteliers or business executives who are currently doing task force work or travel for a living like this type of setup, it is designed to be really exciting. Everyone thinks it is so glamorous, but that is not necessarily the truth. In that case for me, I did have big plans and I did have big ideas. But first was the matter of doing the real work at the hotel in Rockford. I arrived to find a very well-run hotel. The staff was good and they had been there for quite a while. The hotel was originally built in the mid-seventies and had been consistently among the very best of the hotels in our company.

The city of Rockford was similar in size to Denton. I liked the people and I liked the town. At that time, Rockford ranked as the three hundredth best/worst city in the United States to live in. I guess that statistic was based on the economic downturn and other factors used in the ranking. But I really enjoyed myself getting to know the community. I met quite a few of the local people through our accounts at the hotel as well as visiting with the Chamber of Commerce and CVB staff members. Supposedly, Rockford was the basis for the imaginary town of Lanford, Illinois, in the TV series "Roseanne," which was the number one rated TV show in 1989.

Throughout the summer, the trip was everything I could have hoped for. I enjoyed my time up there. I got to see all of my friends. I saw more baseball games than I could have ever imagined while also traveling into downtown Chicago and the lakeshore of Milwaukee many times. The whole area was so beautiful during the summer. It was a magical time to be young on the road. Plus, as many road warriors can attest, living on an expense account is great when you can make your own schedule.

As August was wrapping up, it was time to go home and get back to running my own hotel again in Denton. The lesson there was that you never know when an opportunity might come your way, so if you have the chance, take it. You only live once. Whether traveling domestic or international or day trip or long trip, just go for it. No regrets! I've always said that life is about family, friends, and experiences. Anytime you can put two of those together in the same day, you have had a really good day. Those are some words to live by for sure.

Finishing up the year, my team was changing at my home hotel. We were losing some of the staff members who were now graduating from college or were getting close to graduating. It had been a great ride for two years with almost zero turnover on the front desk, which in today's world would be almost unheard of. I was so blessed by that team. I enjoyed working with them, but change is inevitable. I do remember all of their names and wish I could have stayed in touch with them over the years. They allowed me to grow, and heck, they were the reason I was able to spend the entire summer away from the hotel with minimal help.

I had taken great pride in teaching them everything I knew over that time. Some of them would have made great GMs, but only one of them over that time frame would become an actual hotelier. That person was a young student at the University of North Texas. She had "it" and almost from the beginning, I knew she had great things ahead of her. I hired her some time near the end of 1989 to be a front desk clerk.

Her name is Sandy. She was not originally from Denton, but married a young man from Denton after graduating from college. Sandy has since gone on to an amazing career in the hotel business, currently serving as an executive with a major hotel management company located in the Dallas/Fort Worth area. She was the first person who I had mentored or worked with directly who followed the path into the hotel world. But thankfully, she would not be the last.

Working with all of those young people at that time and teaching them everything I knew would come to be a hallmark of my career. I believed in sharing my knowledge with my team so they would have the opportunity to grow and learn. Some people may believe that they have to "guard their homework" or not tell the people around them what they do or how they do it. To me, that thought process is completely flawed! I would much rather have someone around me or on my team who teaches others and helps them grow, flourish, and develop their own management styles and leadership attributes. Help people become better. Then the world around you becomes better by what you instill in them and develop within them, rather than not sharing what you know. Sharing is caring!

6

1990 – REBUILDING AND PREPARING FOR THE NEXT STEP.

As the New Year began, I was coming into my fourth year as a general manager. Even though 1989 had been terrific, I was hoping that 1990 would be even better. The turnover started to come especially on the front desk, as I had feared. So my time at the beginning of the year was consumed by hiring the new team and training them. I had also started to become much more involved with the Chamber of Commerce and the CVB in Denton. I was evolving as a hotelier and understanding the opportunities to connect through networking events, which would play a pivotal role in my career from that time forward.

At that time, I had also met a young lady through the multitude of events I was attending on a regular basis. I had just turned twenty-four the past October. That young lady also had an October birthday and was twenty-one. But even looking back now, I thought of her as much more mature. The difference in age never really occurred to me when we met. We were just two young people trying to make our way in the world. As we attended different networking events, mixers, and meetings, we seemed to gravitate toward each other, as we were clearly the youngest people at most of those events.

During the summer of 1990, love seemed to be in the air, and ultimately the two of us started dating. It was a wonderful time to be together. She had a great job in Denton semiconnected to the hospitality industry, so we were essentially inseparable. I am sure that any of you in the hotel or hospitality related field can relate. Sometimes only the people in our business understand our business. That may also mean you found your significant other through this crazy world of ours or connected through some type of event related to the business.

Denton had added more hotels over those past few years and the CVB team was doing a great job of bringing businesses to the city. I was asked to be on the board of directors of the CVB, which I thought was a great honor. The other hoteliers in the city had also decided to create a local hotel association, which consisted of fourteen hotels. We had asked Don Hansen, the president of the Texas Hotel and Lodging Association based in Austin to come to Denton and speak to the CVB, as well as all of the hotel GMs. This was my first time to see how the association world worked and the power associations could bring to bear as advocates for their industry. Mr. Hansen was an amazing speaker who could captivate his audience with stories of his time in the hotel industry.

He fascinated me with his knowledge and his connections throughout the hotel industry. The more I learned from him and understood what his job was, the more I was intrigued by that type of job and considered it a great way to give back to the industry. While he was speaking to our Denton hotels, he was focused on how a local association could develop programs for the staff members through meetings and workshops. He and I developed a friendship that would last many years. Whenever I would see him, he would tell me to never underestimate the power of relationships. He always stressed how connections within the hotel business could make all of the difference in the world to my career. He told me if I stayed in the hotel business, I would see the same people for a long time, so never doubt how I could help someone or how someone could help me. He would often say if you lead people, you can change a person's life. Make sure you change it for the better.

The wisdom Mr. Hansen imparted to me, a twenty-four-year-old young man, meant the world to me. It seemed as if he was telling me I would be in the hotel business for a long time. Maybe he saw something in me that reminded him of his career. I have had people help me all along the way of my career, but none of them has had more impact on me than he did. The influence we have with other people cannot be understated. As a result, focus on helping others grow. That will ensure you are always growing, as well, through them. The people you help could be your greatest legacy.

The next big situation that would happen at my hotel and our company was that David, the regional manager from the DFW area, was resigning from the company for another opportunity. He was a good man and I enjoyed working with him. He was subdued, but confident, and certainly knew the hotel business. I was not sure who was going to get the position, but I was really hoping my buddy Jon from the DFW Airport hotel was going to get the job. In my mind, it was his time. He had been in the business at that time for probably fifteen years, which seemed like forever to me. Our company had grown to six hotels. I thought for sure since Jon lived in the area, was local, and knew all the GMs, it was his opportunity to become the regional manager.

Well, as we all know, what you think you see in business may not be what is happening behind the scenes. Apparently as good as Jon was, he was somewhat outspoken and the corporate office had their eyes on another GM for the position. The other guy was Richard, who I had met a few times and I had interacted with him the previous summer. Richard lived near Chicago. He was going to be moving to Madison to work out of the corporate office. Jon seemed to take it all in stride, but since I served in the area of Chicago, Milwaukee, and Madison the previous summer, I had already heard about Richard and his management style. He had a reputation of being almost ruthless to the core with anyone he did not like. He was not outspoken, but was incredibly direct and cutting with his criticisms to his subordinates. None of the people I knew or connected with in the Midwest had anything nice to say about him. But apparently, he wowed the correct people at the corporate office. As we all know, sometimes that is all that matters.

In August 1990, Richard flew down to meet with all of the GMs in Dallas. The GMs in Austin drove up to meet with him. Even though I had not said much to them, they all knew Richard too and were not impressed, to say the least. He seemed to have a Napoleon complex. Someone had wronged him somewhere along the way and now everyone else was going to know for sure that he was in charge. You could not question his authority without paying the price. About the time he started in Texas, Gerri, the GM of the Arlington hotel, resigned her position. She had since gotten married and was having her first child. She did not want to mess around with this Richard guy, so it was time for her to leave. Also, the GM of one of the Austin hotels was leaving, so I felt pretty secure that I would be left alone, at least for the time being. Richard was going to be busy dealing with these issues, so little old me in Denton, Texas, was not going to be on his radar.

Richard leaving me alone was a good thing because I was having an incredible year at the hotel. The new staff had truly settled in after the turnover at the beginning of the year, I was in love with an amazing young woman, and everything was right with the world. But, as we all know, it seems that when you start to hit that steady groove, something is going to throw a wrench your way. Whether you could have seen it or not, it catches you when you least expect it. The unexpected part was going to hit me in early December 1990. As I mentioned, the GM of one of the Austin hotels had resigned. They had replaced him with another GM in September, but that new GM had simply not worked out. Richard called me. By then, I could still tolerate his style, so we were doing okay. As long as I was staying in good graces and out of his way, I figured I was alright with him.

Richard's phone call started out okay. Then he asked me what I thought the next career step was for me, since I had then been at the hotel in Denton for almost four years. I told him I was thinking I would maybe stay in Denton for another year or so, then possibly move to one of the other hotels in the DFW Metroplex. Whether that next hotel was Arlington or Mesquite did not really matter to me because I knew Jon was not going to be leaving the DFW Airport hotel anytime soon. Richard then informed me that the new GM in Austin was not working out and he wanted me to think about moving to Austin to take over that hotel. The Austin hotel was smaller than the Denton hotel, but had significantly more revenue. Plus the Austin market was poised to take off starting in 1991. For those of you in the hotel business or who travel to Austin on a regular basis, think about how busy the Austin market is all of the time. That trend seemed to have started in 1990 and has never stopped.

After the call, I had to discuss the option with my girlfriend and decide if it was indeed time to make the move from Denton to Austin. The next question of course was whether she would go with me or if this was the end of our relationship. She thankfully said she would go. We were going to move to Austin together at the beginning of 1991. It was a sad time for me throughout December, as I was leaving my team behind. I was also leaving behind the many new friends I had made in the area who were connected to the Chamber of Commerce and the CVB.

My mom was happy for me, my friends were happy for me, and everyone at the hotel was excited for me. I knew my team would miss me as much as I would miss them, but it was simply time for the change. I realized at that point, I could not stay at the hotel. I needed a new challenge. Even though I did not know it, the Austin hotel would certainly present its own set of new experiences. Those experiences would allow me to grow a lot. Looking back, this would be one of the many stepping stones of my career that would define me as a hotelier. My girlfriend and I packed up everything we wanted to take with us and on January 7, 1991, we moved to Austin, Texas.

7

1991 – MY FIRST OFFICIAL TRANSFER AS A GENERAL MANAGER.

As I arrived in Austin in early January 1991, the entire hotel was a mess. The GM, who I had known a few years, had been really good from everything I knew and what I had been told. The other GM, who had taken over in September and was recently fired, had damn near destroyed the place in just the past ninety days. It was eye-opening to me because it taught me that a bad leader could destroy a good team very quickly, then someone else had to deal with the fallout of their actions. After the GM had been fired in mid-December 1990, there was an interim manager named Les. Les was trying to put it back together. Les was a GM from one of our hotels in Wisconsin. I really liked him. He certainly knew what he was doing, but it had been an uphill climb for him over the previous few weeks, to say the least. He was really excited to see me when I arrived on the scene to take over.

Les was going to be at the hotel working with me for a couple of weeks. We were working day and night to figure out how to move forward. Most of the desk clerks had quit recently because the other GM from September had been so bad. The clerks simply were not able to take it any longer. Les was hiring new staff members as fast as he could get them in the door. Most of them seemed pretty good. I was trying to get to know them when I would see them during their shifts. A few of these staff members were college students at the University of Texas and a couple of them were looking for extra hours in addition to their real jobs. We were trying to accommodate them. It was like a free-for-all. Get them in and see who stayed. We would sort it all out later.

A few of those new employees definitely had potential for success in the hotel business, but most of them were people who just wanted a job. Thankfully, some of them were willing to work extra hours if needed as we rebuilt the hotel from the ground up. Once Les left to go back to his hotel in Wisconsin, the hotel was officially mine with all of those new people. We were starting to find our connection. I wanted to develop the hotel in the same image as the hotel in Denton. The first thing I had in mind was developing the A/B staffing model on the front desk. I was confident the new front desk employees would be up for it, so we put it in place right away. The team liked it, I liked it, and we were off and running as we rolled into the summer.

One of the strangest things I had to deal with involved Regina, one of our front desk clerks. Regina's mother worked in the house-keeping department and was having an issue with Regina's husband. I was not sure of all the details, but I could tell there was an issue. Regina wouldn't say much to me, but her mom was telling the other housekeepers and the word was getting back to me. Apparently, it was domestic abuse-related. I was not sure what to do about it, and it was getting worse. At some point, it would affect the hotel, but not in the way I thought it would on one particular evening.

Regina called me at home around 8:00 p.m., crying like crazy. I could obviously tell that she was upset. My girlfriend knew about the situation, as I had told her what I felt was happening. As soon as I got the call, she mouthed to me asking if it was Regina. I said yes, it was.

I listened to Regina's story. Her husband was drunk, and she felt he might hit her or worse. She was going to leave him but had no place to go with her daughter, who at the time was a toddler. She did not want to go to her mom's house. She thought I could let her stay at the hotel for the night, which she felt was an option. I was not crazy about the idea, but I was not going to let her down if I could help her out. To get involved in the situation was probably out of my comfort zone. I had a sinking feeling in the back of my mind, but I did it anyway simply out of human kindness.

I called the hotel and told them Regina was coming to the property. I told the desk clerk to give her a comp room and to put the listed name under my name. The desk clerk said he would take care of it, no problem. All of that seemed to go smoothly, given the circumstances, so I went to bed. Regina was safe at the hotel and we would figure out the rest the following day. When I got to the hotel the next morning, Regina and her daughter came down to the front desk around 10:00 a.m. They had most likely stayed up pretty late that night before. She came into my office. I could tell she had been crying even that morning. Of course, she was still upset.

I did not see any visible signs of abuse. If I did, I would certainly have leaned toward calling the authorities. Regina proceeded to tell me about the terrible situation at home. It all seemed to be bad with her husband's constant abuse. She assured me she was going to leave him and get a divorce. She told me she needed some time off of work to get her head wrapped around what to do next. I told her we could of course cover her shifts and to please keep me in the loop as the whole thing moved forward. As she was leaving, I asked her to let me know when she was ready to come back to work. Her job would be there waiting for her.

The conversation went reasonably well given the gravity of the situation. What I have not mentioned is that our hotel had just installed a full surveillance system at the front desk, complete with video and audio. There was a camera behind the front desk and a microphone in the ceiling above the desk hidden in the tiles. It was the brainchild of Richard, who felt it was a good idea to play "big brother" at the hotel to oversee everything that was happening at all times with full video and audio. We were using VHS tapes and the recorder was in the office. A tape would last eight hours. Each front desk clerk was responsible for changing out the tape at the beginning of their shift.

Of course in 1991, there was no internet or website-related surveillance systems. To watch the video, Richard had to come to the hotel and view it during his regular visit to the property. I was fine with the system. Nothing had really popped up when Richard would sit there with a smug look on his face as I watched the tapes with him. He loved to watch the beginning and end of the tapes where there was interaction with the front desk clerks switching out their shifts. Those two situations were about to collide as he came down within a week or so after Regina had stayed at the property. She had "checked in" to the hotel around 11:00 p.m. with her toddler daughter. That was in the time frame of the shift change between the evening desk clerk and the night auditor coming on at 11:00 p.m. I had not even realized that and had no idea a lot of their interaction was on the video tape along with the audio.

As Richard and I sat down to watch some of the tapes, he coincidentally picked that particular day and that particular tape. It was actually the start of the 11:00 p.m. tape. We could clearly see the two front desk clerks talking when Regina walked in with her daughter. Richard started to perk up as he noticed her and quickly figured out it was her, as he recognized her and knew her voice. He looked at me and asked, "What is the deal with this?" From there, it went from bad to worse as I explained the story to him. I had not even thought of it because Regina was on leave for a while and was getting her life together. We continued watching the tape until Regina went to her hotel room about fifteen minutes later. Then Richard started in on me about what I should have done and what I had done wrong.

He gave me fifty questions across all sorts of his theories or thoughts related to the situation. Among them were what was my relationship with Regina, did the staff know about this, had the husband been around, and were we worried about him coming around? Everything you can think of was running through his head at that point. I honestly don't know if he had ever been in a relationship because I never saw him with anyone or heard of him being with anyone. I felt he was way out of his depth with that situation, but you could not tell him that. The next day, he wanted to meet with some of the desk clerks and Regina's mother. I told him that was fine. We could arrange that. I knew I may have been over the line by giving Regina the comp room, but while it was happening, I was trying to help someone in need with the resources I had at my disposal.

The next day, Richard met with a couple of the desk clerks, Regina's mom, and me. Regina's mom was scared to death, wondering why he was investigating the situation. He wrapped up the conversation and came to meet with me. All the while, I was trying to figure out his thought process and where his inquiry was going. He entered my office and closed the door. I was then cleared from any wrongdoing other than giving her the hotel room. But, that guy was so cold and such a by-the-book regional manager that he wrote me up, which was fine. But then he told me I had to fire Regina. His reasoning was even though I made the decision to let her stay, the employee handbook clearly stated an employee could not stay at their own hotel without prior permission from the corporate office. Well, I was obviously not considered a member of the corporate office. I was just the general manager, so she did not have the proper authority to stay at the hotel. Thus, she had to go.

To say I was dumbfounded would definitely be an understatement. I knew I did not like the guy, but now he had entered an entirely different level in my book. I understood the rules. I understood the situation. But, for goodness' sake, my actions may have saved Regina's life that evening. Who knows? I certainly did not think that allowing her to stay at the hotel would get me a write-up and cost Regina her job. Sometimes rules are just a little too strict. The human element may outweigh what someone has written down in an employee handbook with the best of intentions to protect the company. To this day, I have never forgotten that incident and, more specifically, how that whole thing probably affected Regina and her life. I had not used the golden rule that David, my previous regional manager, had told me in 1987, "If you are EVER not sure about what to do, no matter what the situation is, always follow the rules and you will never go wrong." I had not followed the rules and it cost Regina eventually.

Later that year, I noticed one of our housekeepers was doing a great job and always seemed to be interacting with our guests. Her name was Juliana. She was one of the new employees who Les had hired earlier in 1991 after the changeover from the previous GM. I spoke to Marla, our executive housekeeper, about Juliana to see if she knew anything about her and what she thought about her job performance. Marla was very positive about her and told me she was thinking about talking to me about Juliana. I learned that Juliana had grown up in the Austin area. She went to a local high school, but had not graduated for various reasons. She was bilingual, fluent in English and Spanish, and had a wonderful outgoing personality. I thought with her personality she would be a perfect fit on the front desk.

I had already filled Regina's position on the front desk as the full-time morning desk clerk. But in the meantime, one of our part-time weekend desk clerks had given their notice and would be leaving soon. Maybe that would be the perfect opportunity for Juliana to grow within our hotel. She would remain in housekeeping three days during the week, then work on the front desk on the weekends. I spoke to her about her life, her goals, what she wanted to do, and what she thought about working the front desk on the weekends. She was a very likeable person who had all the intangibles of the job: bilingual, outgoing, and incredibly smart. She had needed a job and Les hired her on the spot while he was at the hotel in January. I enjoyed getting to visit with her and I knew she could do the job. She just needed encouragement and a chance. I was going to give her that chance.

I told her that Marla was on board with the option, but it was up to her if she wanted to accept the position on the front desk. She only had to say yes. Luckily, she did say yes, and she started working the front desk that following weekend. We structured her schedule where she would work Wednesday, Thursday, and Friday in housekeeping. Then she would work Saturday and Sunday on the front desk. She was excited to get started. The housekeeping team was as excited for her, since they saw this as a chance for one of their own to move into a different role within the hotel. She trained for the next two weekends and on the third weekend, she was ready to go on her own.

Juliana did an awesome job on the front desk. Just as I was trying to figure out how to get her more hours, our full-time evening front desk clerk gave her notice. Sometimes the best plans fall into your lap. The resignation was that plan coming to fruition for Juliana. She accepted the new position, immediately leaving behind her job in housekeeping for good. The team was happy for her. She remained in that position on our front desk for the next two years. With a smaller hotel like ours, there was not much more she could do for further growth within our company. She did not want to move out of Austin, so the new position was going to be the peak of her opportunities with us.

When she did leave in late 1993, I was sad. But she went to work at a larger full-service hotel in the Austin area on the front desk. I am sure she was promoted within that company or another company along her career path. She was THAT good, so I hope she remained in the hotel industry. I lost touch with her over the years. But I will always remember how I may have helped a young person with desire, drive, and passion to better herself through her hard work.

8

1992 – THE WORST OF TIMES, THE BEST OF TIMES.

As 1991 wrapped up, we were doing some good things at the hotel in Austin and I felt encouraged about the staff I had put in place throughout the year. I'd turned twenty-six the previous October and had finished my fifth full year as a general manager, which definitely meant the hotel business was truly my career path for the foreseeable future. Richard and I were still figuring each other out. I was not a big fan of his, especially after the Regina situation. Some of the decisions he was about to make were really going to annoy me and cause all kinds of havoc with our staff and our guests at the hotel.

Moving into the spring of 1992, the high school state championship basketball games were held in Austin and our hotel was full on Friday and Saturday nights. During that time, the hotel being full each weekend would last until Labor Day. Surprisingly, Austin did not have enough hotel rooms to fill the demand. That trend seems to have continued almost to this day. But, back to Richard and his big idea that he knew was going to increase revenue at the hotel. In his mind, it would not be a problem for anyone, even though it was ultimately a problem for EVERYONE.

The hotel was considered a highway hotel in the business. It was an off-the-road type of hotel located on Interstate 35 on the south side of Austin. In those days, some hotels had a large sign displaying the room rate. The sign was designed so you could literally change the room rate from day to day. It had letters and numbers similar to a movie theater marquee. We would increase the rate every Friday morning from $49.99 to $69.99, then change it back the other way on Sunday morning. The guests had no issue with the rate. There was no internet, no World Wide Web, and certainly no dot-coms such as the online travel agencies we have all become accustomed to. However, Richard decided we could upcharge for the rooms during the week-days by listing the rooms on the sign during the weekdays as "From $49.99."

The hotel had ninety rooms and three floors. His big idea was to price the rooms on the third floor for $49.99, the rooms on the second floor for $59.99, and the rooms on the first floor for $69.99. Today in the hotel industry, we refer to that as revenue management, but it was truly the same concept with his weird by-the-floor idea. In my mind, it was essentially known more directly as "bait and switch," which is the wording I thought of immediately after he told me what he wanted to do.

You would see the room rate on the road sign on the weekdays as "From $49.99." But if you came inside and the rooms on the third floor were sold out (which did happen periodically), a guest could then have a room on the second floor for $59.99 or choose a room on the first floor for $69.99. Richard thought he had reinvented the wheel. Even though there may have been something to the madness, imagine my staff having to explain to guests how it worked. A guest would walk in. We would try to tell them that the room they thought they would get for $49.99 was not available and only the $59.99 or $69.99 rooms were available.

As much as I disagreed with it and could see the frustration with our staff and the guests as it happened day in and day out, he would not change his mind. We were stuck dealing with his "brilliant" idea. Thankfully, back in those days there was no Tripadvisor or Yelp. There were no customer satisfaction surveys. If so, I am sure our little hotel on the south side of Austin would have been crushed by negative guest reviews. Also, if I did not mention it, no other hotels in Richard's portfolio were doing it and no other hotels near us in Austin were doing it. We were all alone as his guinea pig hotel trying to implement his ridiculous program.

What I learned from this is if you are a boss or leader, you have to be aware of how your decisions impact the staff who work for you when you are not there to deal with the ramifications of those decisions. Richard would not listen to me at all. Even though the revenue increased slightly from it, the complaints and the toll on the staff were not worth it in my mind. I kept saying, "Why not just raise all of the rates to $59.99 and install the basic rate structure we are all used to? His direct answer was to get the guests in the door. Then once they had parked and were at the desk, they would not walk out. They would take the room at the rate we gave them.

In spite of him and through sheer will, I was keeping the staff together. We did lose a few staff members who were college students at the end of that spring semester, but our core employees were doing well. I enjoyed working with them. Sadly, we were about to get a rude awakening of how quickly life can take a turn and just what sort of craziness can happen at any hotel or anywhere else when you mix drinking, jealousy, and apparent machismo into the equation.

One particular Wednesday morning in May 1992 was not like any other as it started. We were busy the night before, the staff was working hard, and we were preparing to have a party that Thursday evening for all of the college students who were graduating or leaving us. We were losing three students for the summer. Two of them were hopefully going to come back after the summer, but one was graduating from the University of Texas. We wanted to do something fun celebrating their accomplishment. But, that Wednesday around 10:00 a.m., one of the housekeepers came running down the hallway into my office. She was all shook up, crying, and almost hysterical rambling in Spanish. I tried to calm her down, but she kept saying in English, "Blood, blood, blood." Marla, the executive housekeeper, had by that time also come down to see what was happening.

The housekeeper explained in Spanish to Marla that she had entered a guestroom on the second floor to clean it and there was blood everywhere. She did not see anyone in there, but the blood was on the floor, it was on the walls, and she was scared to death. Marla and I immediately rushed up to the room. We told the housekeeper to stay there in my office. The front desk clerk was tending to her. But now, we had to get up to the guestroom right away. As I opened the guestroom door, sure enough, there was blood everywhere. It was on the floor, on the walls, and it may have even been on the ceiling. I was just trying to take it all in.

I made my way into the guestroom and noticed there was in fact someone in the room. A man's body was on the floor between the two beds. He was face down with the phone cord wrapped around his neck and the cord was stretched down to his legs. It looked like he had been hogtied and had been strangled with the cord. The phone was probably somewhere in the room, but I did not see it in that moment. All I saw was the man lying there motionless and blood was everywhere. It was a very weird scene. It appeared it had been one heck of a struggle or fight and the poor man was on the losing end of whatever had transpired in the room the previous night.

Similar to what had happened at the hotel in Denton, I told Marla not to come in any farther, get out of the room, and call the police immediately. We got out of the room, headed down to the desk, and called 911. The 911 operator asked me if I was sure the man was dead. I answered, "Yes." The operator told me to not go back into the room and the authorities were on the way. It took about three minutes for the first police officer to arrive, then another, another, and another. Then the paramedics and a couple of unmarked cars with what I presumed were detectives also arrived. They came in and asked for me. I escorted them up to the room. As they all walked into the room, even they were taken aback by the scene. It was pretty horrific.

The authorities took over the scene of course and told me to get any information I could about who the man was, who stayed in the room, and any other pertinent information about the situation. They then told me to have our staff watch the side entrances to the building. No one was to come in without permission from the police. I asked a couple of our housekeepers and our maintenance guy to stay at the doors to direct anyone who wanted to come in that they needed to go through the front entrance where a couple of the police officers were stationed. Maybe the police thought whoever had committed that terrible crime was still around and they did not want them coming back or doing any more damage.

I headed back down to the front desk to find out any information I could about the guest. The poor housekeeper who had walked into the room was still in my office. I told her to clock out and go home. We were going to deal with the situation. She could come back the next day. I told her to not worry about it. As it turned out, the room was occupied by two construction workers who were part of a bigger crew that had been staying at the hotel over the past week or so. I had noticed them coming in each evening, but had never seen them departing in the mornings. I guess they were leaving for the job site early each day. Their foreman was a nice guy. We had no problems with any of them until that situation.

The police were working through their investigation upstairs. Around noon, the foreman of those workers came into the hotel to check on his guys who had not shown up for work that morning. Sure enough, there had been the two men staying in the room. Neither had come to work, so the foreman had come back from the job site during lunch to check on them. He came to the front desk and of course saw the police officers everywhere. I came out to greet him. I then directed him to the officers and told them who he was. They took him to the side and asked if I could give them an empty guestroom on the first floor to meet with him. I gave them a room key right away and they disappeared into the room with the foreman. During the next few minutes, the detectives came down and a few more officers went into the room. It seemed after an hour or so I heard them all coming out. I peeked my head out from my office to see what was happening. The foreman left and the officers came into my office.

As they were piecing the whole thing together with the scene, the information we had given them, and the foreman's statements, they were at least able to get a handle on what had happened and told me about it. Apparently, the two men staying in the room, along with the rest of the crew, had gone out drinking together the previous night at a bar. The two men in the room were vying for the affection of one of the young ladies they met in the bar. A fight had started between them, but it had been broken up by the other guys in the crew. None of the crew thought anything about it. They were drinking too much, but it seemed that the two men had made peace at the bar. For them to stay at the hotel in the same room as they had done for the previous week appeared to be no problem.

Over the next few weeks, I learned one of them was in fact the jealous type. He must have not been okay with the peace they had made at the bar, thus continuing the fight back at the hotel around 2:00 a.m. when they got in from the bar. The man who ended up in the middle of the hotel room floor with a phone cord tied around his neck had a car that was stolen by the other guy. That guy had fled to Mexico. He would be found years later in 1995, then extradited back to the United States. The entire situation is so vivid in my mind because when the killer was brought back to Austin, I had to testify at his murder trial, since I was the GM of the hotel during the murder and I was the person who found the dead man lying on the floor. The killer was found guilty of murder at the trial and sentenced to death. Beyond that, I am not sure what happened after he was sentenced because I did not want to keep up with the situation any longer. The sight of all the blood in the room on that day and the poor man on the floor with the phone cord wrapped around his neck was enough for me to deal with.

The summer of 1992 was ending. But my life was about to take an important turn, as I had asked my girlfriend to marry me and we were getting married in August. My buddy Jon, the GM who had really mentored me in the hotel business, was going to be my best man at the wedding. It was such an exciting time for me and my then fiancée. We were planning on having many of our friends from the hotel company come to the wedding, as over the previous five years I had built close relationships with many of the GMs across the company, as well as a few of the leaders at the corporate office. I still could not stand Richard, my regional manager, but the wedding was going to be epic and even though he was going to attend it, my friends were coming down and the entire event was going to be great.

I don't remember exactly what we were thinking, but we did not have a lot of money built up at the time. So we were going to hold the wedding at my fiancée's house and it was going to be an outdoor wedding. For any of you who are from Texas, think about what we were going to do. We were holding an outdoor wedding in Texas in August, where the temperatures routinely get above 105 degrees. But, we did not think about it or consider it. We wanted to have a big wedding with our friends. Because we did not have the money to do much else, we were going to hold the ceremony outside. Well, for whatever reason, someone must have been looking out for us because on that day in 1992, the weather was perfect. The temperature was in the mid-eighties, which may not sound like a break, but trust me, it was an extremely lucky break. We all survived the day and now I was a happily married man.

Nineteen ninety-two ended without much fanfare. I still enjoyed living in Austin and I was starting to make some connections with the other hoteliers in the city, the CVB, and the Austin Hotel and Lodging Association. Austin was growing rapidly, as it always seems to be no matter what era. It was an exciting time for me and my new wife. We loved our friends. Even though I was working way too much, we enjoyed our lives together as the year wrapped up. I was ready for 1993 to begin.

9

1993 – SO BUSY I CAN BARELY KEEP UP.

The recession of the early 1990s had officially ended during the previous year. Our hotel was now incredibly busy, not just on the weekends, but during the weekdays as well. I was begging for an assistant GM, but Richard would not let me hire someone, so I was working a lot of hours. I knew my wife was not happy with the situation. But what could I do? I loved the hotel and it was my career. Unfortunately, I was still the only one in a management role at the hotel. The toll on me and my life was rough. It was even more difficult when the hotel would lose a staff member or have any sort of change at the front desk. Even though I had set up a good system of coverage on the front desk, sometimes I was the one who had to fill in. It was as simple as that.

The summer of 1993 would prove to be an even more difficult situation because we lost our part-time night auditor in April. He was not a student, but a guy who was working on Friday and Saturday nights to earn extra money. We were trying to compensate for his loss. Then the other part-time auditor left as well, all within a two-week period. So, now I was down one position, but two employees, which I had not had to deal with in quite a while. In the meantime, I was the one working every Friday night and every Saturday night on the night audit shift from 11:00 p.m.–7:00 a.m.

Richard still thought I should have been able to work Monday through Friday and even on Friday I should have stayed at the office until 5:00 p.m., just as if it was any other day. I remember having the discussion with him about the schedule and about hiring an AGM. But that was not going to happen, so I was stuck with the situation. He was getting on my last good nerve, but I would suck it up and deal with it, at least for the time being. I ended up working the part-time night audit shift for the next two months before I could settle everything down and get my staff back in order. It was a miserable existence, to say the least. I was none too happy about it. My wife was certainly not happy about it. But it was my job.

The hotel was making almost as much money as any of our other hotels in the company, even though it was the smallest with only ninety rooms. The weekends were constantly full and then we were filling up every Monday, Tuesday, and Wednesday. Our only break in the roller coaster ride of being full was occasionally not filling up on Thursdays or Sundays. The money was literally pouring in as quickly as we could count it. We had raised the rates across the board finally at the beginning of the year. All rooms were priced $79.99 with the weekend rates moving up to $89.99. No one even blinked at the rates. That may not seem like a lot for a room, but at that time, many of the other hotels of similar size and similar type were charging much lower rates, particularly in other cities where our company had hotels.

Thankfully, Richard had finally cut out the lousy "bait and switch" rate structure. Of course, the rate structure change did not take place without a fight. More and more of our guests had been calling the corporate office in Madison to complain about it. Finally, our senior vice president, who was one of my really good friends by that time, had enough of it and told Richard to cut out that stupid idea.

I thought the hotel could not get any crazier after finally settling down the staff and dealing with the murder in 1992, but another day in the life of a hotelier was about to give me an experience that I had not yet dealt with. Laila, our full-time night auditor, was a seasoned hotelier. She had been in the business for more than twenty years at that time. She was great at her job. We connected because we liked the numbers aspect of the hotel. Plus she was a hawk in finding errors, then correcting them for me before I had to deal with them. She had worked at one of our competing hotels down the road, but I hired her away in early 1991. She was a huge help to our team and almost like a mother to some of the other employees when she would see them at the changeover of shifts at 11:00 p.m. for the evening desk clerk or at 7:00 a.m. for the first shift clerk.

As I mentioned previously, the night auditor at many hotels is the only person who is on duty during their shift and thus, responsible for the entire building for eight hours from 11:00 p.m.–7:00 a.m. Laila was great and I never doubted she could handle anything thrown at her. But she was about to really be put to the test in the middle of the night in late July. With no cell phones and only pagers for the GMs at that time, the staff seemed to have no problem contacting me if they had a question. I don't believe we had caller ID at that time, but if the phone rang at my house, I could almost guarantee it was someone at the hotel needing something. It drove my wife crazy, as I am sure it does many of the significant others of hotel or hospitality professionals who have to deal with it even to this day. The calls can come in at any time, day or night.

Laila was usually pretty good about not calling me in the middle of the night, even if she needed me. She would wait until maybe 6:00 a.m. or 6:30 a.m. to reach out, as she knew I was probably awake by that time in the morning. With her shift ending at 7:00 a.m., she sometimes wanted to touch base with me before she left the hotel. So, when the phone rang at 2:00 a.m. on that particular July night in 1993, I immediately popped up. It scared the bejeebers out of my wife, but I was wide awake the moment I answered the phone. I had always had that keen sense that when the phone rings in the middle of the night, you had better be ready to roll because it is almost always going to be something you need to deal with right then.

That time, as I picked up the phone, all I could hear was the very loud fire alarm going off from the other end of the phone. It was Laila calling me from the hotel. The fire alarm was going off and there was a fire at the hotel. All I could get out of my mouth was to call 911 and I was on my way. Again, my poor wife by then was wide awake as well and asked me what was happening. I said, "There is a fire at the hotel and I have to go." I was out the door in about a minute. We lived about fifteen minutes from the hotel. I made it there in what felt like five minutes. As I arrived, there were already about four fire trucks, two ambulances, and maybe six police cars there. I plowed through the back parking lot, parked, and ran inside the building to see what was happening. Were any guests impacted? What was Laila doing and how was she?

I met with a policeman at the front door, explained who I was, and tried to determine what had happened. He directed me to what must have been one of the lead firefighters, who told me one of our hallway air conditioners on the first floor had caught on fire. It was all contained in that small area. No guests were impacted from what he could tell. The firefighters had it under control at that time. That was a relief, so I headed back to the front desk. Laila was there. Even though she was reasonably shaken up, she seemed to be okay. I then followed the firefighters down the hall so they could show me where the fire had occurred and what they felt may have caused it.

Somehow the fan motor of the AC unit had frozen up. For whatever reason, there was a spark or ignition source that then caught fire within the mechanism. It is still not sure how that happened. I never saw it happen again. I have dealt with that type of AC wall unit throughout my career, so it was a once-in-a-lifetime glitch that happened to us. Another unusual thing that we had to deal with that night was a guest who simply would not answer his door during all of the commotion. Of course, all of the guests had been awakened by the fire alarms going off for maybe fifteen minutes or so, except for that one guest. It was a room on the second floor. Even though the firefighters had been banging on the door, the guest would not answer and the deadbolt lock was in place.

Around 3:00 a.m., the firefighters came to get me. They wanted to check on that guest, so they asked me if I could come up and find out what was going on with that room. I rushed up there and knocked and knocked, but to no avail. Still no answer. I was thinking, "Oh Lord, please do not let us find someone dead in the room because I am about to get the deadbolt key and go into the room." We could not get an answer, so I told the firefighters, "I will be back in a minute," then I headed downstairs to get the deadbolt key to figure out what the problem is with this guest." As I came down to the front desk, Laila yelled out to me the guest had called her. He was okay and he wanted us to stop knocking on his door. I said, "Well, why is he not answering the door?" She said she did not know. But he was fine and he wanted us all to go away and not bother him anymore. I never did figure out what the deal was with the guest. But we left him alone for the rest of the night.

I had survived my first fire at a hotel, we had survived the unexplained strangeness of that guest, and Laila would end up being with me as our full-time night auditor for the remainder of my time in Austin. But, during those few hours after I was awakened in the middle of the night and had dealt with that guest in July 1993, my heart rate had probably never been as high or my stress level that intense for just those short bursts when my mind was thinking, "what could be wrong?" I am sure everyone can relate to that part of their job. Not knowing is always the worst feeling you ever have to deal with.

In October, my wife's grandparents wanted to come down and visit with us to celebrate our birthdays. My wife's birthday was in early October and mine was in late October. They wanted to drive down from Denton and spend the weekend with us in the middle of the month to celebrate both birthdays. They had not been to Austin in a while, but it sounded like a good idea and we were both excited to see them. My mom had been down periodically, and my wife's parents had also come down to see us. But her grandparents coming down was going to be something special. They drove down on a Friday afternoon. They had already lined up where they wanted to eat and where they wanted to go for the entire weekend. All of that sounded great. I knew my wife was excited to see them and spend some time with them. I had arranged to have the weekend off from the hotel.

The weekend started great. We had a wonderful dinner that Friday night. It was a fun time visiting with them. They were staying at the hotel. Even though I was technically "off," my wife and I would of course come to the hotel to pick up her grandparents and go out for the day, as we did that Saturday. Saturday had been an incredibly fun day. We got to see some of the places they wanted to visit. I knew my wife was really happy that they had come down. As we arrived back at the hotel that Saturday night to drop them off around 9:00 p.m. or so, I realized there were police cars in the parking lot. There were not a lot of police cars, but a couple of them, so I immediately thought something had happened. The hotel had not paged me or reached out, so hopefully the situation would not be too bad to deal with.

I walked into the hotel to find a couple of police officers standing in the lobby and another one was behind the desk with Jeffrey, the front desk clerk. It was apparent to me that there had been some type of struggle or wild situation, as there was a man in handcuffs sitting in the lobby next to one of the police officers and there was shattered glass all over the lobby. The hotel had a glass barrier at the front desk that covered the entire desk. At night, you could close it and interact with the guests through a small tray. It was not as weird as it may sound. It was probably designed to keep someone from jumping over the desk or trying to rob the hotel with a knife. The front desk clerk could escape to the back office if there was that type of situation.

But, in this case, something had definitely happened. As I mentioned previously, there was a full audio and video surveillance system at the hotel covering the front desk area, so I would discover what had occurred. As I walked in, my wife took her grandparents up to their room so they did not have to be around that mess. Then I was able to deal with the situation. I introduced myself to the police officers and then walked behind the desk to speak with Jeffrey. He had been with us a few months and was our 3:00 p.m.–11:00 p.m. front desk clerk on Saturday and Sunday evenings. He was not a college student, just a young man maybe in his late twenties who was looking for a part-time job on the weekends. So the position at the hotel fit him perfectly.

Even though I did not see Jeffrey often because of the shift he worked and my hours during the week (earlier in the summer when I was stuck working the night audit shift on Friday and Saturday nights), we had gotten to know each other fairly well during the changeover of our shifts. He seemed like a well-rounded young man who had his head on straight. There had never been an issue between him and another employee, much less a guest of the hotel. That was all about to change once I got behind the desk that evening as he proceeded to tell me the guest (the man in handcuffs in the lobby) had come at him and was disrespecting him.

The guest had gotten so angry that he had pushed the glass panel at the front desk out of its tracks. When it fell back, it had shattered all over the desk and the lobby floor. This was Jeffrey's story and the one he had also told the police officers. About that time, one of the police officers asked if I had access to the surveillance system, since they had already seen the video camera behind the front desk. I said, "Yes, I can get into it for you and we can watch the whole thing unfold in real time. Let me set it up in my office for all of us to watch."

While I was setting it up, I pulled out the VHS tape from the video recorder and plugged in the monitor, which was in my office. All the while, Jeffrey was saying, "He started it, he started it." I told him to calm down and we would work it all out. Even the police officers had to tell him to calm down. I put in the tape and rewound it to the moment where I can still see that there was glass at the front desk. I knew it was prior to it being destroyed. We watched the video and it became painful to watch as the guest came up to the front desk. He was definitely drunk or under the influence of something because he was slurring his speech. At the same time, he was being somewhat belligerent toward Jeffrey.

Jeffrey was having none of this. Even though he may have been able to deal calmly with the guest, the whole thing escalated pretty quickly. The guest had locked himself out of the room he was staying in and could not remember which room it was when he went down to the vending machine area to get a soda. He had come back to the front desk to get a key to his room after realizing he did not know for sure what room he was in and had started the guessing game with Jeffrey.

To Jeffrey's credit, he did not give him a key to the room because this guy was not listed as a guest and he was simply guessing which room he was staying in. He actually could not remember the name of the guest who was registered in the room. The whole ordeal was somewhat bizarre to watch on the video. I kept thinking there was a way this could have been solved, but ultimately it just blew up. What happened next was Jeffrey and the guest started yelling at each other.

Jeffrey had clearly had enough of the back and forth because he raised his voice to an entirely different level. Jeffrey proceeded to tell the guest he had better get the "F" out of the hotel and if he did not leave, Jeffrey was going to call the police on him.

During their exchange, a few other choice words come out from both sides. The whole situation spiraled out of control even further. The guest started pushing on the glass at the desk. With a really hard push, the glass came out of its tracks, landed on the desk, and shattered all over the place with a thunderous crash. At this point in the video, it almost appeared that Jeffrey was going to jump the desk counter and go after the guy. But even though Jeffrey had crossed over the line interacting with the guest, he did not pursue the guy in the lobby. As you heard the call unfold, he called the police while the guest was still yelling at him. The police arrived and immediately cuffed the guest, which is the scene I had walked in on with my wife and her grandparents.

Once we watched the tape, Jeffrey was still proclaiming his innocence. The police then asked if we wanted to press charges. I said, "Yes, we do" and they took the drunk guy away in handcuffs. Then I met with Jeffrey for a little while. By now, the other desk clerk, our part-time night auditor, was there for his shift that started at 11:00 p.m. I told Jeffrey that his behavior was way over the line and unacceptable. What came over him to go crazy on the guy, even though the guy was clearly a drunken idiot? He said he had been dealing with a lot of stress at his other job during the week and the guy just hit him at the wrong time with the wrong language. He was not going to take it anymore.

I asked him if he wanted to continue working at our hotel because that type of conduct was certainly not what the hotel/hospitality business was all about. He told me he liked working at the hotel, but admitted that he was probably not the right guy to continue in the position and needed to focus on his other job. He told me he would come back to work his shift on Sunday from 3:00 p.m.–11:00 p.m., since he knew my wife's grandparents were in town. But that would be it for him and he felt it was best if he resigned.

I often think about the Jeffrey situation from that night. As any hotel/hospitality professional can attest, there are many days when guests truly push you to your limit and more. I am sure that also applies to other jobs or careers. But in our industry, people sometimes feel like their boundaries or limits of civilized interaction are thrown out the door once they walk into a particular establishment. In other words, it is the establishment's responsibility to put up with whatever the guest, patron, or customer is throwing at them. In the hotel world, you cannot imagine what some of the hotel rooms look like after guests have destroyed them. This runs the spectrum from simply a messy room to blood or body fluids everywhere to complete destruction of the room with anything and everything broken and food all over the floor, walls, and every place in between. I am not sure why people think someone else is simply going to clean up their mess and they are entitled to destroy property because they are paying for the privilege of staying in a hotel room for the night.

10

1994 – IS THERE LIGHT AT THE END OF THE TUNNEL?

By the time 1994 rolled around, I was still enjoying Austin, but the job was taking a toll on me and certainly taking a toll on my marriage because Richard would not budge on giving me any extra help or an assistant GM for the hotel. The hotel was still incredibly busy with no end in sight. I thought there was no light at the end of the tunnel. The hotel market was doing great and occupancies were through the roof. I used to tell my friends at the corporate office we should either build another hotel or buy an existing one. The corporate office was not interested in expanding but I am certain in the years since then, the hoteliers who did end up building hotels in Austin or taking over existing ones knew I was on the right track. Even back in 1994, Austin was an incredible city in which to be a part of the hotel business.

There had been more staff changes at the end of 1993. I liked the new staff members. A fresh beginning in 1994 was hopefully what I needed to re-energize myself because for the first time, I was starting to hit the burnout zone. I am sure most hoteliers or for that matter anyone in their job hits that wall. You either fight through it or decide to leave the job and move on. As most statistics say, people may not quit their job, they simply quit their boss. As my boss, Richard was wearing pretty thin on me and my life at that point. His management style was certainly souring my love of the hotel industry. I was not sure how much longer I could take him, even though I loved else everything about the business and our company.

In addition to building strong relationships with my staff during that time, I also developed a very close professional and personal relationship with Darren, our senior vice president. He was such a good man who I thought highly of, due to his wisdom and insight in the hotel industry and overall business knowledge. He was Richard's boss and, as much as I did not want to get into that issue with Darren, at some point, either Richard or I would have to go. Darren's wife had actually been one of the bridesmaids in my wedding in 1992. I was an usher in his wedding and my wife was a bridesmaid in his wedding. We were close. I felt I could confide in him because Richard was just pushing me too hard.

Luckily, other circumstances would intervene, allowing me a break from Richard. I would survive the ordeal of him being my boss. I even told Darren my innermost thoughts on Richard's management style. I felt he was essentially a conniving manipulator who Darren should be leery of because someday he could backstab Darren. That theory would be proven correct in only a few years. Sure enough, Richard would backstab all of the people I cared about at the corporate office and take over the company, only to run it into the ground within a few years after he took over.

Some circumstances intervened on my behalf. The company made some changes in the areas that each regional manager had under their jurisdiction. Thankfully these changes would save my job with the company, at least for the time being. In the summer of 1994, Richard was assigned to a different area in the Midwest. Another regional manager was going to be my boss. The new regional manager was Perry, who had actually been with the company almost since the beginning in the early 1970s. I was excited to have him take over as my boss and get Richard off my back. I had gotten to know Perry a little when we would see each other at the company meetings twice a year in Madison.

He was a nice guy, very by the book, and I do mean by the book. He would never veer off the path from the direction of the company or the direction he was given by Darren. His management style was incredibly boring, but he got results and you knew where you stood with him at all times. He was a straightforward, no-nonsense type of leader. I really did not care what his style was as long as Richard was gone. Perry was the guy. I was all in on getting to know him better, since I had to work with him. Almost four years of Richard had taken its toll on me, but now there was in fact light at the end of the tunnel. It would come in the form of a new boss, thank goodness.

Perry and I were doing fine getting to know each other as the spring of 1994 rolled into summer. But once again, a horrific event would happen at the hotel that would definitely shape the direction of my career, even though I did not know it at the time. Laila was still with me as our full-time night auditor. She was doing great, as was the rest of our staff. They were so glad to have the old me back, since the departure of Richard had truly re-energized me.

The hotel was located on the south side of Austin. It seemed like there was an increase in gang activity starting to happen around the area. I was not sure why this was happening. It could have been the growth of drugs in the area or just our hotel's time to have to deal with it. It had gotten so bad that on the weekends, we had security each Friday and Saturday night from 7:00 p.m. until 7:00 a.m. There was a considerable cost involved with the security strategy, but Perry was on board. He knew we needed to do better protecting our guests and our staff members.

Things seemed to be calm, but on one Thursday night in the summer of 1994, that was all about to change. During the day, a room had been rented on the second floor by an individual. There was nothing unusual about that, but apparently this individual was a known gang leader. And by known, I mean the police knew it and the community may have known it. But we did not, and to our staff, he was just a guest, no different from any other guest. Later that evening, another room was rented to a guest on the third floor.

Sadly, unbeknown to us and our staff, that other room was rented by a guest who was also involved with a gang, but not the same gang that now had a room on the second floor. This had all happened within a few hours, as the third floor room was rented around 10:00 p.m. The front desk clerk who rented the room to the guest on the third floor was the only staff member on duty. There was no security, since it was a Thursday night. Actually, on this evening, I remember after the fact it was a relatively slow night for the hotel. Our occupancy was probably no more than sixty percent that night.

Laila, the night auditor, came into work at 11:00 p.m. just like she had for the past couple of years. She had survived the fire in 1992. She was such a big help to me and the staff, but this night would test the limits of everyone's tolerance for what we deal with in the hotel business. Once again, we did not have cell phones. We only had pagers. The hotel used a phone to connect with the GMs. That particular phone call was one I will never forget. As I tell this story, I remember the next few hours of that incident as if it happened yesterday.

The phone rang at my house around 1:00 a.m. It was Laila, who was screaming in my ear that there had been a shooting at the hotel. The police were on the way, and I needed to get there as soon as I could. I rushed out of the house and headed over to the property, similar to when I had rushed over during the fire in 1992. I arrived very quickly. There was a flurry of activity in the parking lot. The police, fire department, and paramedics were there. It seemed like the SWAT team was also there. It wasn't really the SWAT team, but a few of the police officers who were dressed in tactical gear with long weapons. They were surrounding the building.

As I got out of my car and ran toward the hotel, I could see Laila behind the desk. I tried to make my way through the officers to get inside and figure out what was happening. The officers escorted me into the building. Laila was shaken up as they started to tell me what was going on. Apparently, the people in the gang on the second floor realized there was another gang on the third floor. These groups did not like each other. The story was a feud had been brewing and it was not going to end well.

As the situation played out over the next few days and weeks, this is what happened, according to the authorities. The gang on the third floor (Gang 3) had brought in some guns to the hotel through the side doors, and they were going to sell these guns to some other people. Our hotel had been chosen as the place to do the transaction because of its proximity to Interstate 35, its quick access on/off the highway, its having side doors, and its having no security on the weekdays. Sadly we were the perfect choice for that type of transaction. The meeting for the sale of the guns was set for midnight. The gun sale went off without a hitch right at midnight.

However, the coming and going of Gang 3 had somehow raised the suspicions of the gang on the second floor (Gang 2). No one was quite sure how they ran into each other with each being on different floors, but the two groups were about to get into a deadly altercation. Gang 3 had a few guns left in their arsenal. One of them was a shotgun. When the two groups had some sort of interaction, Gang 3 went down to the room of Gang 2. They figured out one of the gang leaders of Gang 2 was in that room and they wanted to either scare him or literally start shooting up the room.

Gang 3 knocked on the door of Gang 2's room and went inside. There was some sort of scuffle or fight and Gang 3 dropped their shotgun in the chaos. Gang 2 picked it up and was about to start shooting. The Gang 3 members started scrambling for their lives to get out of the room. Gang 3 made it out of the door by some miracle without getting shot all to heck. The guest room door closed. Gang 2 chased Gang 3 down the hall. The last member of Gang 3 to escape the room was just about to make it to the stairwell when he was shot. Two shots rang out down the hallway that night. One of them found its mark on that young man. The autopsy revealed he had been hit in the head with two pellets from the shotgun. He was dead within seconds, if not immediately after he was struck. He was only eighteen years old. His younger brother, who was with him, was only seventeen. He had been fortunate enough to be one of the gang members to escape and make it out of the building alive.

The whole scene that evening was chaotic. Though the police tried to control it, some family members of the dead young man showed up and the media showed up. It turned into a full-on circus. I would guess as the situation played out through the night and into the morning, there were almost twenty law enforcement officers in and around the building. They included, of course, the Austin Police Department, the FBI's gang unit, and the Drug Enforcement Administration. They were piecing together information related to the gun transaction. The authorities seemed to have the whole thing figured out within a few hours. They picked up some of the people involved right away after identifying the young man who had been killed. They did not, however, find the murder weapon that evening. In a very weird twist, the gun would be found by a guest of ours who was out walking their dog behind the hotel almost a year after the shooting happened.

It was such a dramatic situation, I called Perry at home around 6:00 a.m. to tell him what had happened, what was happening, and where I thought the whole thing was going. He was very matter of fact. He said, "Give the authorities anything they need, give them the contact information for our corporate office, and assist in any way you can. Also keep me in the loop as the morning plays out." Poor Laila had now been through a fire in 1992 and murder in 1994. To her credit as a terrific night auditor, she was a trouper and was back at work the following Sunday. The rest of the staff was shaken because when the housekeeping staff arrived that morning, there were still law enforcement authorities everywhere. All we were told by the authorities was no one was allowed to go into the guest rooms involved and no one could go on the second floor hallway where the young man had been shot. Guests who had been impacted or knew what happened slowly left the building. No one seemed to ask a lot of questions, which I thought was weird. Maybe they just had places to be that particular day.

The detectives and the police were working on the second floor after the young man had been taken out of the building. They needed me up there. I was not sure what their intention was, but they needed some dark drapes to cover up the windows on the second floor to ensure that entire hallway was as dark as we could make it, since daylight was showing through the windows. I said, "Sure, I can help out and get you some drapes or something to cover up the windows. No problem." I had no idea why they were doing this, but I was about to find out. That was their CSI type of moment. They said I could stay up there to see it if I wanted to watch.

The police were trying to identify the blood spatter from the victim and were going to use Luminol to trace the blood in the carpet of the hallway and along the walls. Apparently Luminol is a chemical that will glow when it touches blood or somehow has a reaction when it interacts with blood. The authorities use it to trace blood spots or blood spatters at a crime scene. The whole ordeal was a sad thing to witness because, of course, I realized what all of that meant. It was, however, a fascinating experience to have a front row seat watching this all play out. We covered up the windows for them. Then the hallways became pitch black dark. The police sprayed the Luminol and turned on their black light. Sure enough, the blood spots started showing up brightly, as if they were under the black light on a neon poster.

I hoped to never be at a hotel again where Luminol was used because from that moment forward, I could only visualize the episode from that day in 1994. Even when I would go through Marriott or Hilton Quality Assurance inspections later in my career and the inspector would use a black light in the bathroom checking for whatever it is they loved to check for, I could not go through the black light part without thinking of that young man who lost his life at our hotel in that hallway.

The summer rolled into the fall that year. Another life-changing event was about to happen that had nothing to do with the hotel business. My wife and I were expecting our first child, who would be born in May 1995. When I had originally arrived in Austin at the beginning of 1991, I really loved Austin. My wife did not like it, but by the time 1994 was coming to an end, she loved it and I was starting to hate it. Perry had been great to work for so far as my regional manager, but I believed my time at the hotel was coming to an end in 1995. I just had to figure out how to get out of there. I also felt the area was definitely getting more dangerous and I did not want to live there to raise my child in that environment. My dilemma was whether to stay with the company that I loved so much or venture out to another opportunity with a different hotel company. My wife was all over me to make a change and take a leap of faith with another company. However, by that time in 1994, I had been with my company for nine years and did not want to leave them. I just needed to figure out how to leave the hotel.

11

1995 – TIME TO COME HOME AND MOVE ON.

The situation and the area around the hotel in Austin had definitely become more dangerous, so as 1995 started out, I knew I was going to have to leave. The first thing I wanted to do was reach out to Darren, the senior vice president who was then a really close friend. My thought was to tell him I just could not stay in Austin any longer and needed to get out of there. I had been there for four years and done everything they had asked of me. But with a daughter on the way, what could they do to possibly get me back home to the Denton hotel?

After going back home for a few days over the holiday season in 1994, I had come up with the idea to possibly do a switch with Cindy, the GM at the hotel in Denton. She had taken over there as GM in early 1992. She was not the original GM who had come to the hotel after I left at the beginning of 1991, but she seemed to be doing a good job. Actually, some of my old staff members who were still at the hotel liked her. She was from Austin. I thought if I could approach her to "trade" or "swap" hotels, she might go for it. She would be closer to her family and I could get back to mine, allowing my wife and me to raise our daughter in the north Texas area.

As I reached out to Darren in February, we had a long, heart-to-heart discussion. I was brutally honest that I was burned out, semi-scared to have my daughter grow up in Austin at that time, and I wanted to get back home. He was very empathetic. My idea of a "swap" with Cindy was not completely out of the question. The company had actually done something like that before, and it had worked out well for all parties involved. Darren said he was going to run it by Perry, my direct boss, at their next meeting at the corporate office to see what Perry thought. But as far as he was concerned, that would be fine with him. Later that next week, Perry called me to follow up on the situation and see how we could make it work because Cindy had actually thought about the same idea. She had a daughter who was maybe nine or ten years old at the time and her daughter was missing her family in Austin.

Every once in a while, a plan or idea falls right into a place where you hope it will fall. Thankfully, our plan was turning out to be one of those situations. We discussed it further over the coming weeks and everyone came to the consensus that the "swap" would happen. The change was set to officially take place on Monday, April 17. I would first go to Denton to do a crossover change with Cindy and get my stuff up there the following week. We will make the change in Austin for her to take over my hotel. It was all great news. My wife was happy, my family was happy, and my friends in Denton were happy. We were coming back home.

The transition did go according to plan, actually better than expected. My team in Austin was sad to see me leave that hotel, but they were happy for me. I knew they would miss me and I would miss them as well. Some of the employees at the hotel in Denton were still there from when I left in 1991, so to get back and work with them again was going to be a blessing during the year. I felt rejuvenated when I got back to the hotel in Denton and just as comfortable as an old worn glove. I was where I needed to be, as my wife and I were about to welcome our daughter into the world with our families around us. Our daughter was due in early June, but that would change, as she arrived on the scene on Wednesday, May 17, 1995.

The summer was good. Perry was still my regional manager. He had all of our hotels in Texas under him, so the switch from Austin to Denton did not disrupt that part of the equation. I enjoyed working for him. Again his management style was so incredibly boring, but he was thoughtful and had a lot of wisdom from the business. However, a really weird situation would occur in July 1995 that would definitely put the two of us on different paths. Even as the situation was happening, I thought it was not right. I feel the same way after all of this time has passed and with many years to reflect on it. I was just sad it played out the way it did. In the end, the whole episode meant nothing in the grand scheme of things to either one of us, the hotel, or the company, but it would set me on my path to leave the company that I loved so much.

A guest had stayed at the hotel and left behind some sort of personal item. I honestly cannot remember what it was, maybe a dress, a watch, or shoes. It probably doesn't matter, but we were dealing with getting the item back to her. The housekeeping team had found the item the day the guest had left the hotel and turned it in, just like they were supposed to. When the guest phoned the hotel after realizing she had left the item behind, our staff told her we had it and we would mail it out to her. That is where the situation started to go sideways. The guest had phoned the hotel a few days after her stay. She called sometime in the evening and the night front desk clerk had not conveyed that the guest had called inquiring about her lost and found item that we had in our possession. About two weeks later, Perry called me, not the guest. He told me that some guest was yelling at him saying that we had not mailed her item to her. I told him truthfully I knew nothing about it. I was sorry, but we would research it and I would get back to him right away.

We were trained that if a guest left an item behind at a hotel, DO NOT call the guest to inform them that they had left something behind. That policy was in place because someone other than the guest might answer the phone or if you leave a message, someone other than the guest might hear the message. You can put two and two together here, as the premise was you do not reach out to a guest to let them know you have their lost item. Maybe that guest was not supposed to be at your hotel and may have been there with someone they were not supposed to be there with. You get the picture. That was our policy, so we had not reached out to that particular guest. She had in fact reached out to us, but I was completely unaware of that fact. We had truly dropped the ball along the way. I was not lying to Perry when I said I knew nothing about it. I promised him that we would get the item out to her right away. He said, "No problem." The issue was resolved. Well, I thought the issue was resolved.

Sure enough, we found the item. In the meantime, the front desk clerk who had taken the phone call from the lady remembered the conversation. He told me he must have gotten busy that evening when she called and forgotten to relay the message or make a note for me. I told him, "No problem. We have it now and we are going to get the item back to her." The item in question was relatively small. I remember putting it in a box and sending it back to her via the U.S. mail. Actually, our mail person had picked it up that next day. We had it boxed up nicely. We felt we knew how many stamps to put on it. It was on its way back to her, problem solved. At least that is what I thought.

A couple of weeks went by and Perry called me again. He was somewhat agitated, as the lady had called him again, saying she still did not have her lost and found item. I told him that was not possible. We had mailed it out to her at least two weeks before. He said, "Well she does not have it. What is the issue and did we put a tracking receipt on it?" We had not put a tracking receipt on it. I just wanted to get it out to her, and did not even think about it, as it was such a small item. What was the issue with the delivery? That was not what happened. I was being questioned about when I sent it out and how much postage I put on it. The whole dang thing had become a fiasco because the lady left one small item behind in her hotel room in Denton, Texas. I told Perry again, "I know we sent it out and it should be there." He told me to follow up with the mail person the next day to see what I could find out.

Sure enough, I followed up with our mail person, who kinda remembered the situation and the box. He told me to contact the post office and see what they knew about it. I did that. They were not much help, since we did not put a tracking receipt on the package. Darren called me the next day because the crazy lady had gotten ahold of him. She let him have an earful about the ordeal and how the GM in Denton was not sending her that lost and found item. I told Darren the same thing I told Perry. He told me to just find out where the item was and get the damn thing to her so she would get off the corporate office team. I promised him the same as I had Perry. We had sent it and were researching it.

I could not find out anything about the package, but I was keeping them in the loop. They were dealing with the guest when, low and behold, the thing finally showed up at her house. It was then about a month after the fact. I don't know what happened to it, where it went, or what the issue was. Thank goodness she had her item back and we could move on. That was not exactly what happened. As simple as that seemed, the guest had mailed back to Perry at the corporate office in Madison part of the box we used to ship out her item. Apparently the date on the box when it was scanned or ran through the postal system showed at least two weeks after I was claiming that we sent out the item. She was calling me a liar and told Perry that I was holding her item all of that time.

Perry was starting to doubt me and/or my integrity. We were about to have a real problem because I could not convince him otherwise regarding the circumstances of the situation. He came to the hotel shortly thereafter and brought the damn piece of the box with him to show me what she had sent him. Sure enough, what she sent him was in fact part of the box I had put together to send her the item. Unfortunately, the processed date was much later than when I had said we sent it out. I could not explain it, my staff could not explain it, and neither could my postal worker, who had been running our route for as many years as I could remember. It was a fluky deal. Perry would not let it go, which I thought was weird. We had worked together so well over that past couple of years, but I felt he believed I was lying to him. Sadly, that was what he did think. Darren called me a few weeks later and said basically, "Perry is having an issue with this whole package thing and feels you lied to him about it." As much as I professed my innocence, I was never able to convince Perry of the truth. I know what happened on my end. But this situation was going to change my career path because once you have a boss who doesn't believe you or trust you, the game is over.

With that issue not having a good ending and putting me in a precarious position with Perry, regrettably, I thought I needed to start looking for a new job beyond my beloved company and friends. In early August 1995, I started looking for a new job. My wife was actually pretty excited. She thought my current company was not growing, which was true, and she was not sure where my career path was. It was no longer with the company.

For the first time since August 1985, about ten years prior, I started searching the newspaper to look for a job. I saw a few different ads looking for general managers, but nothing stood out. It wasn't until

September that I came across an ad one Sunday morning looking for "Area Director of up to twelve hotels across the DFW Metroplex and into Oklahoma with a dynamic hotel management company based in Fargo, North Dakota currently expanding into the Texas market with rapid growth needing committed, experienced hoteliers right away." That was the content of the ad as much as I can remember. The moment I saw it, I was hooked. In my mind, I felt that I could run multiple hotels as an area director or regional manager or whatever they called it. I knew the job, as I had seen my peers enter that role with my current company. I knew I needed to get my resume to those people in Fargo, North Dakota, and see what they were all about.

My wife helped me with my resume, which had not been updated at any point over those past ten years. I was basically starting with a clean slate and going in an entirely different direction with that new job opportunity. We completed my resume. It was sent overnight to the Fargo people the next morning via FedEx. I was not going to mess with the postal service on that opportunity or worry about my resume getting lost along the way to the corporate office of their management company.

It seemed to take forever for them to respond. I had actually called them a couple of times over that time period. They had received my resume and they would get back to me when they had the chance. That was not necessarily a rousing reception, but I felt I was in the mix. They had the resume in their hands, so let's see how it started to play out. I did call them again one more time, but was unable to reach Julie, the person I had been talking with in the HR/recruiting department. That was all about to change. Julie called me in October to see if I would be available for an interview. Lance, their regional vice president, was coming to the DFW area later that month and wanted to meet with me if I had time. Somewhere in between, I had to go through a personality profile interview with an outside company.

Apparently that interview had gone fine, so I was all set to meet with Lance in late October to have an in-person interview for the area director position.

Julie had told me Lance was staying in Arlington for a few days while he was in town and meeting him at his hotel would be best for his schedule. How did that sound to me? Of course, I told her, "No problem. I can be there and will be happy to meet with him in Arlington." It was all set. I was scheduled to meet him at 7:00 p.m. on that Thursday in October 1995. He was a nice man, not very talkative, about my age, and maybe slightly older. We hit it off right away. I liked him and certainly liked what he had to say about his company. The company had started out as a small hotel company in the Midwest, but they were growing like crazy, now expanding into Texas with their first hotel just being finished in Bryan/College Station. They were hoping to build as many as seventy hotels throughout Texas in the coming years. That was very intriguing to hear because my current company only had six hotels in Texas and a total of thirty-two throughout the United States.

Lance and I must have talked for well over two hours during the interview just going over the plans for their company. I felt it was a really good interview, considering that I had not been through an interview on that side of the table in ten years, much less interviewed for a job with the potential that one appeared to have as an area director with a growing company like theirs. One thing that was intriguing was their company had a plan and they appeared to be on a track to stick to the plan. They would possibly grow to become the largest independent hotel management company in the world. This was all pretty amazing. I was all in after hearing it. I was thinking, "Just let me know what the next step is, then sign me up."

He told me that he would be back in touch within a week or so, but definitely before Thanksgiving, as the holiday season was approaching quickly. My wife was excited as those events were unfolding, but I knew it would mean leaving my friends from the company I was currently with. Perry and I were still not doing well. That crazy lost and found fiasco would not die in his mind. I felt really badly about it. I had done everything correctly with sending the lady her package, but he simply did not believe me. As I look back on that time, I probably should have sent the lady a thank you gift because without her insane obsession to get me in trouble or whatever her motive was, I may never have taken that next step. Sometimes the writing is on the wall to make a change. We simply cannot see it or refuse to believe it.

I had heard back from Lance just before Thanksgiving. He said they were still working on a few things, but I should not lose hope. He would get back to me the first week of December. I told him that was fine and we would catch up at that time. True to his word, he did call me that first week of December and told me his plans. They wanted to hire me to come to work for the company. He would be back in the DFW area the following week. Could I meet with him to discuss the options and go over their plans? That was great news. I immediately called my wife. She was ecstatic of course, but it also hit her that we would be leaving the company where honestly by this time, she too had made quite a few friends.

Lance came down the following week, gave me his plan, and explained how it would all work out in the coming weeks and months going into 1996. He was not going to offer me the position as area director. Rather he wanted me to open the hotels in Lewisville, Texas, as GM. Then we could figure out the next opportunity. He sold it that they were growing so fast they needed seasoned GMs to help get those first few hotels open. After that, those newly hired GMs would probably be the next group of area directors hired in Texas. It wasn't exactly what I wanted to hear. But I knew I had to leave my current company and this opportunity would not come around again. So I would do it. I was going to accept the new job.

I reached out to Darren a few days later to tell him about my plans because he was the one I wanted to speak with first. I would get in touch with Perry the following day. I was not sure if he would be relieved that I was going to be leaving or what his mindset truly was at that point. I really did like him and hated that our relationship had soured to the point where I was leaving this company that had taught me everything I knew about the hotel business. I knew Darren was sad to see me go as well. But the time had come to leave the nest and try to grow beyond all of those amazing people.

I spoke to Lance shortly thereafter and accepted the job to go to work for the new company. My last day with my current company would be Friday, January 12, 1996, and my first day with my new company would be Sunday, January 14, 1996. The plan was to fly to Fargo and start my career with those new guys. I landed in Fargo on that Sunday evening. The real temperature on the ground was two degrees above zero. I had flown that afternoon from DFW where the temperature was a balmy seventy-eight degrees. Yep, Toto, I was no longer in Kansas or Texas. I was ready to start the next chapter in my career. It had been an amazing ten years in "the life of a hotelier."

LIFE LESSONS ALONG THE WAY

This was a ten-year snapshot of my hotel career. I had grown from a young man looking for a job to a veteran of the hotel industry through many different circumstances. I often think of the people who I have described in the book. Even though their real names were changed, they each left an indelible mark on me. I had learned early on the value of relationships and connections. My mom had been instrumental by instilling in me the simple Golden Rule, "Do unto others as you would have them do unto you." Sometimes the simple act of being kind gives you every opportunity to grow a relationship.

I found out quickly the hotel industry can have connections at every turn. If you stay in the industry for any length of time, people may cross your path at one point in your career and later at another point. The employee you hired while you were the boss may end up being your boss with another company if you each happen to change jobs along the way. The old adage of "never burn a bridge" applies tenfold, as people within the hotel industry say they are one degree of separation from each other. Everyone knows everyone, or at least everyone knows someone the other person knows.

I was very blessed during my first ten years in the hotel business to have people assist me, connect me, or just be there at the right time for me. I learned that you can always grow and always learn. Sometimes the best lessons are not what you learn "to do," but what you learn "not to do." I was very young when my career started and people took a chance on me. I have never forgotten that lesson and have always tried to understand that I could be the person helping someone else during their career or as they start their career.

The many twists and turns of my interactions with the employees and guests always gave me insights into people and their actions. Some of the stories in the book were life changing for me, as I am sure they may have been life changing for the other individuals who were involved. I always wanted to assist people where I could or where my authority would allow me to as a general manager of a hotel.

I also learned to be involved in the many associations or organizations of the hotel industry. They always provided educational or networking opportunities and opportunities for growth. In my later years of my career in the hotel industry, I was blessed to be the CEO of a local hospitality-related association in the Dallas area. One of the most important things for me within that association was to ensure everyone knew the value of always learning and developing relationships with the other folks in the association.

Someone reading this book may be in a position to inspire, motivate, or nurture other people they know. It may be as simple as a giving a peer some encouragement or a boss showing their team best practices of certain procedures. Everyone has value, everyone has something to offer, and everyone can be a part of your career or life along the way. Never UNDERVALUE anyone!

I hope you enjoyed the book and it resonated with you at some level. These stories were the good, the bad, and the unbelievable. My next book, *The Life of a Hotelier (The Regional Manager Years)* will give you an even more in-depth look at the hotel industry from someone overseeing multiple hotels.